T0088182

THE LITTLE GREEN BOOK OF

IRISH WISDOM

THE LITTLE GREEN BOOK OF
IRISH WISDOM

DERMOT MCEVOY

Skyhorse Publishing

Copyright © 2014 by Dermot McEvoy

All Rights Reserved. No part of this book may be reproduced in any manner without the express written consent of the publisher, except in the case of brief excerpts in critical reviews or articles. All inquiries should be addressed to Skyhorse Publishing, 307 West 36th Street, 11th Floor, New York, NY 10018.

Skyhorse Publishing books may be purchased in bulk at special discounts for sales promotion, corporate gifts, fund-raising, or educational purposes. Special editions can also be created to specifications. For details, contact the Special Sales Department, Skyhorse Publishing, 307 West 36th Street, 11th Floor, New York, NY 10018 or info@skyhorsepublishing.com.

All images © Thinkstock Photos

www.skyhorsepublishing.com

10 9 8 7 6 5 4 3 2

Library of Congress Cataloging-in-Publication Data available on file

ISBN: 978-1-62636-562-9

Printed in the United States of America

This book is dedicated to

—Who Else?—

The Irish

Acknowledgements

Thank you to Michael Coffey for his help on Irish poets, both obscure and famous.

A special thank you to Rosemary Mahoney for her immense help on the "Writers & Poets" chapter.

And a tip of the hat to the writers who contributed to Chapter 10 Kitchen Table Philosophy: Maureen Dowd, Mary Kenny, Rosemary Mahoney, Alphie McCourt, and Peter Quinn.

Contents

Introduction

Who, exactly, are the Irish?

Well, they are redheads, ink-haired and towheads. Freckles and blue eyes abound. They are descendants of Vikings, Normans, lost Celts, and, according to DNA, in my own family, Bedouin Arabs—probably via Spain and the Spanish Armada. Edmund Spenser, the bigoted English poet, thought them to be descendants of Scythian stock from far Iran, perhaps explaining the term "Black Irish." They are mostly white, but with a sprinkling of black, Asian and Indian. They are largely Catholic, secondarily Protestant, with Jews, Hindus, and Muslims. They are, without a doubt, a mutt of a people.

They are freedom fighters (the British call them "terrorists"), slave-owners, master politicians, relentless defenders of their religions, gay, straight, liberal, reactionary, victims of famine, and mercenaries in the name of imperialism. They are expert

Introduction

businessmen, singers, outlaws, movie stars, writers, poets, priests, highwaymen, beggars, gypsies, gangsters, and athletes. They are drunkards, teetotalers, sexually modest, sexually extravagant, and always shocked by the whole thing.

Their island was called Hibernia by the Romans, Ireland by the British, and *Eire* by their 20th century revolutionaries. Their biggest export is their people, mostly to the United States, but to every country and every continent except Antarctica—although we haven't DNAed the penguins lately.

They are inspirational and infuriating. They are funny and they are cynical. They are extraordinarily talented and remarkably venal. They are tough, adaptable, and the ultimate survivors. They have a deep mistrust of people, but can turn sentimental with a few drops of the *uisce beatha*, translated from the Irish Gaelic as "the water of life"—whiskey—which they invented.

Their names permeate every part of everyday life around the world: John F. Kennedy, Chaim Herzog, Mother Jones, Michael Collins, Edmund Burke, William Butler Yeats, Barack Obama, Frank McCourt, Kathy Griffin, Barry Fitzgerald, Molly Bloom, Liam Neeson, Oscar Wilde, James Joyce, President Mary Robinson, Whitey Bulger, Senator Joe McCarthy, Lady Gregory, Tommy Makem, Senator Eugene McCarthy, Seamus Heaney, Augustus Saint-Gaudens, Saint Patrick, Billy the Kid, Ronald Reagan, Ronnie Drew, Paul McCartney, Sean O'Casey, John J. McGraw, Bing Crosby, Mariah Carey, Whitey Ford, Rev. Ian Paisley, Liam Clancy, Casey Stengel, Francis Bacon, "Wrong Way" Corrigan, Eamon de Valera, George Bernard Shaw, Jimmy Cagney, Maureen Dowd, John Ford, Spencer Tracy, Mayor Jimmy Walker, Eugene O'Neill, Paul Ryan, General Philip Sheridan, Oliver Goldsmith, George Carlin, Charles Stewart Parnell, Tug McGraw, Leopold Bloom, Al Smith, Denis Leary, Archbishop "Dagger" John Hughes, Stephen Colbert, Samuel Beckett, Lord Mayor Robert Briscoe, the Duke of Wellington, and Brendan Behan, just to name a few.

As you can see, "Irish juxtaposition" is a terrifying thing.

They are bewildering. They are infuriating. They may be the most fascinating race of people on the face of the earth. Whatever they are, there is a certain wisdom to it all.

They are impossible—they are the Irish.

Turn the page; get infuriated.

1

Irish on the Irish

"If it was raining soup, the Irish would go out with forks."
—Brendan Behan

• • •

The Irish have a world-wide reputation for being fighters. So much so that it's even stated in the Irish National Anthem, Amhrán na bhFiann: *"We're children of a fighting race/That never yet has known disgrace." And the people the Irish like to scrap with most— this side of the British—are themselves. There's an old saying that if there were three people left in the whole world and they were all Irish, two of them would be off by themselves—talking about the third guy. The Irish are also known as great "begrudgers"; their motto should be "Other people's success should always be challenged!"*

They are a people who mightily take offense—and, if they're lucky—hold them until the day of death! The definition for "Irish Alzheimer's"? They forget everything—except the grudges. A tough race, but tougher on themselves.

• • •

"There's one word that sums up [Hollywood director] Jack Ford and the Irish: MALICE!"
—JAMES CAGNEY

• • •

"Malice is only another name for mediocrity."
—PATRICK KAVANAGH, POET

• • •

"No man is thoroughly miserable unless he is
condemned to live in Ireland."
—JONATHAN SWIFT

• • •

"An Englishman thinks seated; a Frenchman, standing; an
American, pacing; an Irishman, afterward."
—AUSTIN O'MALLEY (1858–1932), PHYSICIST

• • •

"The quiet Irishman is about as harmless as a powder
magazine built over a match factory."
—JAMES DUNNE

• • •

"The Irish people do not gladly suffer common sense."
—OLIVER ST. JOHN GOGARTY

• • •

"Yes, ruling by fooling, is a great British art with
great Irish fools to practice on."
—JAMES CONNOLLY

• • •

"Just because you're born in a stable doesn't mean you're a horse."
—DUKE OF WELLINGTON, DUBLIN BORN
AND NOT PROUD OF IT

• • •

A foreign journalist interviewed Samuel Beckett: "You are British?"
"Au contraire!" replied Beckett, a Dublin-born
Protestant who spent his last 50 years in France

"There was once an Irishman and Jew, and here he is."
—ROBERT BRISCOE, THE JEWISH LORD MAYOR OF DUBLIN

• • •

"Being Jewish in Ireland was not our only cultural conflict.
Being Irish in England was another."
—CHAIM HERZOG, DUBLINER WHO BECAME
THE 6TH PRESIDENT OF ISRAEL

• • •

"My mother is Irish, my father is black and
Venezuelan, and me—I'm tan, I guess."
—MARIAH CAREY, CHANTEUSE

• • •

"The problem with being Irish…is having 'Riverdance'
on your back. It's a burden at times."
—RODDY DOYLE

• • •

"I'm Douglas Corrigan. Just got in from New York, where am I?"
—"WRONG WAY" CORRIGAN ON HIS ARRIVAL IN DUBLIN ON A
SOLO AIRPLANE FLIGHT IN 1938, 6,000 MILES FROM HIS STATED
DESTINATION OF CALIFORNIA

• • •

"It's a big con job. We have sold the myth of Dublin as a sexy place incredibly well; because it is a dreary little dump most of the time."
—RODDY DOYLE

• • •

"An Irishman can always see both sides of an argument, provided it will lead to a fight."
—J. P. DONLEAVY, NOVELIST

• • •

Who better to comment on the Irish than Brendan Behan, Russell Street, Northside Dublin:

"Other people have a nationality. The Irish and the Jews have a psychosis."
—FROM *RICHARD'S CORK LEG*

"It's not that the Irish are cynical. It's simply that they have a wonderful lack of respect for everything and everybody."

• • •

Definition of the "Anglo Irish": "A Protestant on a horse."

"Being Irish, he had an abiding sense of tragedy, which sustained him through temporary periods of joy."
—WILLIAM BUTLER YEATS

• • •

"My father was totally Irish, and so I went to Ireland once. I found it to be very much like New York, for it was a beautiful country, and both the women and men were good-looking."
—JAMES CAGNEY

• • •

"I had to have some balls to be Irish Catholic in South London. Most of that time I spent fighting."
—PIERCE BROSNAN

• • •

Irish on the Irish

"I once saw a sign on a lift in Dublin that said:
'Please do not use this when it is not working.'"
—Spike Milligan, comedian

• • •

George Bernard Shaw, writer, Synge Street, Dublin:

"I showed my appreciation of my native land in
the usual way—by getting out of it as soon as
I possibly could."

"Ireland, sir, for good or evil, is like no other place under heaven,
and no man can touch its sod or breathe its air without
becoming better or worse."

"Put an Irishman on the spit, and you can always
get another Irishman to turn him."

"If you do somebody in Ireland a favor,
you make an enemy for life."
—Hugh Leonard

• • •

"I'm Irish. We think sideways."
—Spike Milligan

• • •

"In Ireland the inevitable never happens and
the unexpected constantly occurs."
—Sir John Pentland Mahaffy

• • •

"Ireland is the old sow that eats her farrow."
—James Joyce, A Portrait of the Artist
as a Young Man

• • •

"Dublin University contains the cream of Ireland:
Rich and thick."
—Samuel Beckett

• • •

"Baloney is flattery laid on so thick it cannot be true,
and blarney is flattery so thin we love it."
—Bishop Fulton J. Sheen

• • •

"The problem with Ireland is that it's a country full of
genius, but with absolutely no talent."
—Hugh Leonard

• • •

"We are one of the great stocks of Europe.
We are the people of Burke; we are the people of Grattan;
we are the people of Swift, the people of Emmet,
the people of Parnell. We have created most of the

modern literature of this country. We have created
the best of its political intelligence."
—W.B. YEATS, IN AN IRISH SENATE DEBATE, JUNE 1925

"When anyone asks me about the Irish character,
I say look at the trees. Maimed, stark and misshapen,
but ferociously tenacious."
—EDNA O'BRIEN

• • •

"When St. Patrick drove the snakes out of Ireland, they swam to
New York and joined the police force."
—EUGENE O'NEILL

• • •

"Whenever I wanted to know what the Irish people wanted, I had only to examine my own heart and it told me straight off what the Irish people wanted."
—Eamon de Valera

• • •

"You know it's summer in Ireland when the rain gets warmer."
—Hal Roach, comedian

• • •

"That's the Irish all over—they treat a joke as a serious thing and a serious thing as a joke."
—Sean O'Casey

• • •

"If one could only teach the English how to talk, and the Irish how to listen, society here would be quite civilized."
—Oscar Wilde

• • •

"There's no point in being Irish if you don't know the world is going to break your heart eventually."
—Daniel Patrick Moynihan, commenting on the assassination of President Kennedy

• • •

"There is something about the Irish that knows that to live is to be hurt, but we're still not afraid to live."
—US Vice President Joe Biden

• • •

Irish on the Irish

"My heritage has been my grounding,
and it has brought me peace."
—MAUREEN O'HARA

• • •

"Intolerance has been the curse of our country."
—JAMES LARKIN

• • •

"My wife and I both come from Irish families. There are two
kinds of Irish families: the hitting kind and the kidding kind.
If you're fortunate—and both of us are—you come from the
kidding kind of Irish family."
—P. J. O'ROURKE

• • •

"We are the music makers. We are the dreamers of the dream."
—ARTHUR O'SHAUGHNESSY (1844–1881), POET

Frank McCourt, writer, Limerick City:

"When I look back on my childhood I wonder how I survived
at all. It was, of course, a miserable childhood: the happy
childhood is hardly worth your while. Worse than the ordinary
miserable childhood is the miserable Irish childhood, and worse
yet is the miserable Irish Catholic childhood."
—FROM *ANGELA'S ASHES*

"Mick of the Month. That's what I am. I'm a Mega-Mick."
—ON HIS CELEBRITY

"Being Irish is very much a part of who I am.
I take it everywhere with me."
—COLIN FARRELL, ACTOR

• • •

"Irish Americans are no more Irish than
Black Americans are Africans."
—BOB GELDOF, ROCKER AND HUMANITARIAN

• • •

"I feel more Irish than English. I feel freer than British,
more visceral, with a love of language. Shot through
with fire in some way."
—KENNETH BRANAGH, ACTOR

• • •

"We save our rhythm for the sheets, not the streets."
—JOE FLAHERTY, JOURNALIST, UPON WITNESSING THE IRISH
MARCHING IN THE ST. PATRICK'S DAY PARADE

John Millington Synge, author, Playboy of the Western World:

"There is no language like the Irish for soothing and quieting."

"The grief of the keen is no personal complaint for the death of one woman over eighty years, but seems to contain the whole passionate rage that lurks somewhere in every native of the island."

"History of Ireland—lawlessness and turbulency, robbery and oppression, hatred and revenge, blind selfishness everywhere— no principle, no heroism. What can be done with it?"
—WILLIAM ALLINGHAM, IRISH POET, DIARIST

• • •

"Ireland is where strange tales begin and happy endings are possible."
—CHARLES HAUGHEY, FORMER *TAOISEACH*

• • •

Irish on the Irish

"It's difficult for an Irishman to apologize."
—ERROL FLYNN AS CAPTAIN BLOOD

• • •

"Never shake hands with the devil until you meet him!"
he advised his companion-on-the-road. "Paddy," replied
the stranger, "*I* am the devil!"
—FROM AN OLD IRISH FOLKTALE

• • •

Broken Irish is better than clever English.
—IRISH SAYING

• • •

"We are, to be sure, a strange lot."
—THEOBALD WOLFE TONE,
18TH CENTURY IRISH REVOLUTIONARY

2

What the Rest of the World Thinks of the Irish

"No Irish Need Apply."

• • •

To say that the Irish have a chip on their shoulder is like saying that Guinness brews a lot of stout. Driven from their own land by poverty and famine, they ended up in other peoples countries and felt the wrath of discrimination. In Boston they encountered the shibboleth that would torture them like a raw wound: "No Irish Need Apply." And the Irish in strange lands continued to bewilder. They were either lovers of freedom and rights, or they were bigots of the worst kind. They were industrious, or they were thieves and murderers. The world saw them as a feral people that were feared before they could ever be loved.

• • •

"The Irish is one race of people for whom
psychoanalysis is of no use."
—SIGMUND FREUD

*George Washington on Ireland's support for
America during the revolution:*

"Ireland, thou friend of my country in my country's
most friendless days, much injured, much enduring land,
accept this poor tribute from one who esteems thy worth,
and mourns thy desolation."

"When our friendless standards were first unfurled, who
were the strangers who first mustered around our staff?
And when it reeled in the light, who more brilliantly
sustained it than Erin's generous sons?"

"Not in vain is Ireland pouring itself all over the earth. Divine
Providence has a mission for her children to fulfill; though a
mission unrecognized by political economists. There is ever a
moral balance preserved in the universe, like the vibrations of
the pendulum. The Irish, with their glowing hearts and reverent
credulity, are needed in this cold age of intellect and skepticism."
—LYDIA M. CHILD, AMERICAN ABOLITIONIST

• • •

"We have lost America through the Irish."
—Lord Mountjoy

• • •

"We have always found the Irish a bit odd.
They refuse to be English."
—Winston Churchill

• • •

"When Irish eyes are smiling, watch your step."
—Gerald Kersh, British writer

• • •

"The Irish are a fair people; they never speak well of one another."
—Samuel Johnson

• • •

"The Irish are a race of people who don't know what they want
and are prepared to fight to the death to get it."
—Sidney Littlewood, British lawyer

• • •

"The Irish do not want anyone to wish them well; they want
everyone to wish their enemies ill."
—Harold Nicolson, British author

• • •

"The Irish are not at peace unless they are at war."
—George Orwell

• • •

"The Irish seem to have more fire about them than the Scots."
—SEAN CONNERY

• • •

"For the great Gaels of Ireland/Are the men that God made mad/For all their wars are merry/And all their songs are sad."
—G.K. CHESTERTON, "THE BALLAD OF THE WHITE HORSE"

• • •

"Yes, I am a Jew, and when the ancestors of the Right Honourable Gentleman were brutal savages in an unknown island, mine were priests in the Temple of Solomon."
—BENJAMIN DISRAELI IN RESPONSE TO AN ANTI-SEMITIC TAUNT OF DANIEL O'CONNELL

• • •

"Perhaps no class of our fellow citizens has carried this prejudice against color to a point more extreme and dangerous than have our Catholic Irish fellow citizens, and no people on the face of the earth have been more relentlessly persecuted and oppressed on account of race and religion than have this same Irish people. The Irish who, at home, readily sympathize with the oppressed everywhere, are instantly taught when they step upon on our soil to hate and despise the Negro. They are taught that he eats the bread that belongs to them."
—FREDERICK DOUGLASS

• • •

3

Religion: God Save Ireland (Because it's the Least He Could Do)

"We are a nation of believers.
We produce anti-clerics, but atheists, never."
—WILLIAM BUTLER YEATS

• • •

During the Troubles in Belfast there was a joke circulating.
A gunman goes up to a man on a dark street and says, "Are you
a Catholic or a Protestant?" "I'm an atheist!" replies the terrified
man. "So," responds the gunman, "are you a Catholic atheist or a
Protestant atheist?" The moral of the story might be that religion,
no matter how heavy the denial, is never very far away in Ireland.

Ireland, since the arrival of transplanted Protestants in the early 17th century, has always been tormented by religion. Let's face it, religion is like a stigmata on the Irish psyche. From the Protestants you'd hear "No Pope Here!" From the Catholics: "The hell with King Billy and God bless the Pope!" The 2011 census showed the Catholics in the Republic still out-populating the Protestants by the count of 84% to 3%, while the census for Northern Ireland showed the Catholics and the Protestants tied at just about 41%. But as Bob Dylan once said, "The Times They Are A-Changin'" as witnessed by the success of the Good Friday Agreement. Also, the young are not as caught up in the extreme bigotry or clannishness of years past. There is a place for all religions on the island, although Ireland will probably be always known for its Catholicism, even as that Catholicism diminishes by the year, reserved mostly it seems, for baptisms, marriages and burials. While Catholics remain the majority, the imprint of Protestants on the culture of Ireland cannot be denied. Three of the four Irishmen who won the Nobel Prize in Literature have been Protestant (Yeats, Shaw, Beckett), with Seamus Heaney being the lone Catholic. And if not for the Protestants of the United Irishmen—men like Wolfe Tone, Lord Edward Fitzgerald and Robert Emmet—the nationalist revolutionary movement may have been stillborn.

The apogee of the Catholic Church was the visit to Ireland of Pope John Paul II in 1979. After that the public's support for the Church began to wane for several reasons, one being the Church's opposition to birth control. Another was the Church's adamant position against divorce. Also, for the first time the question of abortion was being broached, raising the political temperature, as the Church obsessed on the subject. Moral authority demands the high ground and the Church lost it as reports about the clergy sexually preying on young boys surfaced. That was bad enough; but when cover-ups by Church officials were revealed, the blow to the Church was substantial, if not mortal. Diarmuid Martin, the current archbishop of Dublin, had this to say:

"It is likely that thousands of children or young people across Ireland were abused by priests in the period under investigation and the horror of that abuse was not recognised for what it is. The report will make each of us and the entire church in Dublin a humbler church."

The involvement of the Church in cahoots with the government in the Magdalene Laundries—institutions where as many as 30,000 young women were often confined for life on minor (often sexual) offenses—evoked a firestorm of protests, and an apology from the Taoiseach, Enda Kenny:

"Therefore, I, as *Taoiseach*, on behalf of the State, the Government and our citizens, apologise unreservedly to all those women for the hurt done to them, and any stigma they suffered, as a result of the time they spent in a Magdalene Laundry."

The Catholic Church has taken a severe beating in Ireland. As church after church closes it becomes apparent that you can take the church out of Ireland, but is it really possible to take the Church out of the Irish?

"I am Patrick, yes a sinner and indeed untaught;
yet I am established here in Ireland where I profess
myself bishop. I am certain in my heart that 'all that I am,'
I have received from God. So I live among barbarous tribes,
a stranger and exile for the love of God."
—SAINT PATRICK

• • •

"We have just enough religion to make us hate, but
not enough to make us love one another."
—JONATHAN SWIFT

• • •

I saw God. Do you doubt it? Do you dare to doubt it?
I saw the Almighty Man. His hand
Was resting on a mountain, and
He looked upon the World and all about it:
I saw him plainer than you see me now,
You mustn't doubt it.
—JAMES STEPHENS, FROM "WHAT TOMAS
AN BUILE SAID IN A PUB"

• • •

"I am a pious apostate, an atheist shocked by the faithlessness
of the believers, a fellow traveler of moderate Catholicism
who has been out of the church for 20 years."
—MICHAEL HARRINGTON, AMERICAN SOCIALIST

• • •

"It doesn't say anywhere in the Constitution this idea of the
separation of church and state."
—SEAN HANNITY

• • •

"There's no reason to bring religion into it. I think we
ought to have as great a regard for religion as we can,
so as to keep it out of as many things as possible."
—SEAN O'CASEY, *THE PLOUGH AND THE STARS*

• • •

"It is undoubtedly true that until the prejudices of the Protestant
and Unionist minority are conciliated… Ireland can never
enjoy perfect freedom, Ireland can never be united."
—CHARLES STEWART PARNELL

Bernadette Devlin, socialist politician:

"Among the best traitors Ireland has ever had, Mother Church
ranks at the very top, a massive obstacle in the path to equality
and freedom. She has been a force for conservatism…to ward
off threats to her own security and influence."

"One American said that the most interesting thing about
Holy Ireland was that its people hate each other in the
name of Jesus Christ. And they do!"

"Once you attempt legislation upon religious grounds,
you open the way for every kind of intolerance and
religious persecution."
—WILLIAM BUTLER YEATS

• • •

"God is a concept by which we measure our pain."
—JOHN LENNON

• • •

"The whole patriarchal, male-dominated presence of the
Catholic Church is probably the worst aspect of all
the establishment forces that have sought to do
down women over the years."
—MARY ROBINSON, FUTURE PRESIDENT OF IRELAND

• • •

"The Bible was a consolation to a fellow alone in the old cell.
The lovely thin paper with a bit of mattress stuffing in it,
if you could get a match, was as good a smoke as
I ever tasted."
—BRENDAN BEHAN

• • •

"I can't bring up my kids in a church whose authority system
is entirely based on the size of fucking hats, okay? That's
apparently how the Catholic Church is run. The bigger
the hat, the more important the guy, right? Priests have
no hats, cardinals have those little red beanies, the pope
has a collection of big hats... God must have a huge fucking

sombrero up there in heaven! 'Look at me, I'm GOD!
Look at the size of my hat, who else would I be?'
I don't know, lead singer of Los Lobos?"
—DENIS LEARY

• • •

"We used to say that we could not trust an Irish parliament
in Dublin to do justice to the Protestant minority. Let us take
care that that reproach can no longer be made against your
parliament, and from the outset let them see that the Catholic
minority have nothing to fear from a Protestant majority."
—EDWARD CARSON, UNIONIST

*Sinéad O'Connor has the voice of an angel—and the bite
of a wolfhound when it comes to the Catholic Church.
A magnet for controversy, in 1992 she caused a national
ruckus when she tore a picture of Pope John Paul II in
protest on* Saturday Night Live *because of the sexual
abuse being perpetrated by the Catholic Church.*

"As long as the house of The Holy Spirit remains a
haven for criminals the reputation of the church will
remain in ruins."

"When you live with the Devil you learn there's a
God very quickly."

"My story is the story of countless millions of children whose families and nations were torn apart for money in the name of Jesus Christ."

"If you were the boss of a company and some of the employees of your company were known to sexually abuse children, you would fire them instantly."

"I think there's a difference between God and religion."

Bishop John Hughes became New York's first Archbishop in 1850. He was nicknamed "Dagger John" because of the stiletto-like crucifix he wore. Some, however, say it was because of his sharp opinions. He was born in County Tyrone in 1797 and immigrated to America 1816. He was in charge of the New York diocese beginning in 1842 and his tenure coincided with the great influx of Irish immigrants fleeing the Great Famine. He was so alarmed by the Protestant institutions of the day that he set up his own Catholic alternatives, including schools, hospitals, and orphanages. He was also the founder of Fordham University, Manhattan College and Marymount College. It was also under his tutelage that the construction of St. Patrick's Cathedral began.

"I am an American by choice, not by chance. I was born under the scourge of Protestant persecution, of which my fathers in common with our Catholic countrymen have been the victim for ages. I know the value of that civil and religious liberty, which our happy government secures for all."

"We shall have to build the schoolhouse first and the church afterward. In our age the question of education is the question of the church."

"The Catholic Church is a church of discipline."

The "Know Nothing Party" organized Protestants to march on Old St. Patrick's Cathedral. Hughes wrote to New York Mayor James Harper warning him that "Should one Catholic come to harm, or should one Catholic business be molested, we shall turn this city into a second Moscow," meaning he would burn the city to the ground, à la Napoleon. Incidentally, no harm came to the Cathedral or to Hughes's parishioners.

Edmund Burke, although dead for over 200 years, remains a daily presence in Dublin City as his statue, along with that of dramatist Oliver Goldsmith, guard the front gate of Trinity College at the foot of Grafton Street. The statesman is beloved by both conservatives and liberals for his opinions which contain a lot of common sense, something that remains uncommon to this very day.

"Religion is essentially the art and the theory of the remaking of man. Man is not a finished creation."

"Religious persecution may shield itself under the guise of a mistaken and over-zealous piety."

"Nothing is so fatal to religion as indifference."

"What ever disunites man from God, also disunites man from man."

"You can preach a better sermon with your
life than with your lips."
—OLIVER GOLDSMITH

• • •

*Comedian George Carlin was born in Harlem [he called it
White Harlem, which he said sounded tougher than saying
"Morningside Heights"] and attended Cardinal Hayes High
School—until he was expelled. As a performer he brought a
certain Irish zaniness to his act, but his fierce intellectualism
was deadly as he attacked institutions, politicians,
wars, and the injustices of society.*

"I would never want to be a member of a group whose symbol
was a guy nailed to two pieces of wood."

"I'm completely in favor of the separation of
Church and State. My idea is that these two institutions
screw us up enough on their own, so both of them
together is certain death."

"Atheism is a non-*prophet* organization."

"Religion is just mind control."

What matter that at different
shrines/We pray unto one God?
—THOMAS DAVIS, NATIONALIST

*Bishop Fulton J. Sheen was one of the most popular radio
and television hosts of the 20th century. His show "Life Is
Worth Living" in the early days of television served to
introduce Americans to Catholic thought in a time when
many Catholics in the United States were thought to be
nefarious agents of the Pope by their Protestant neighbors.
He won two Emmy Awards as Most Outstanding Television
Personality. There is presently a movement afoot
to have him canonized a saint.*

On winning his Emmy: "I feel it is time that I also pay tribute
to my four writers, Matthew, Mark, Luke, and John."

"Hearing nuns' confessions is like being stoned
to death with popcorn."

"An atheist is a man who has no invisible
means of support."

"I'm an Irish Catholic and I have a long iceberg of guilt."
—EDNA O'BRIEN, WRITER

• • •

"In order to find his equal, an Irishman is forced to talk to God."
—BRAVEHEART, SPOKEN BY DAVID O'HARA,
PLAYING STEPHEN

• • •

"Intellectually I resisted [Catholicism], but though
logic stripped away the cant and ceremony,
I still could not rid myself of the voodoo."
—BOB GELDOF

• • •

"Let me pray to God…The bastard! He doesn't exist."
—SAMUEL BECKETT, ENDGAME

• • •

"Love is never defeated, and I could add, the
history of Ireland proves it."
—POPE JOHN PAUL II

• • •

"Wear a Condom—Just in Casey"
—SLOGAN ON T-SHIRTS THAT APPEARED IN DUBLIN AFTER
BISHOP EAMON CASEY ADMITTED TO FATHERING A SON

• • •

"Man is born broken. He lives by mending.
The grace of God is glue."
—Eugene O'Neill

• • •

"Isn't an agnostic just an atheist without balls?"
—Stephen Colbert

• • •

"The bishops will govern the Church, the priests will do all the
work, and the deacons will have all the fun."
—Richard Cardinal Cushing,
Archbishop of Boston

• • •

"I sometimes think that God in creating man somewhat
overestimated his ability."
—Oscar Wilde

• • •

"Now that he's a Catholic, perhaps he'll become a Christian."
—Daniel Patrick Moynihan, on the baptism of
columnist Robert Novak

• • •

"My mom always said that if the Protestants catch a Catholic
in their church, they feed them to the Jews."
—Kate O'Brien, writer

• • •

"The Puritan has passed; the Catholic remains."
—WILLIAM CARDINAL O'CONNELL,
ARCHBISHOP OF BOSTON

• • •

"Faith is what someone knows to be true,
whether they believe it or not."
—FLANNERY O'CONNOR

• • •

"He died of a poisoned altar boy."
—JOE FLAHERTY, JOURNALIST, ON THE DEMISE OF
FRANCIS CARDINAL SPELLMAN, THE REPUTEDLY
GAY ARCHBISHOP OF NEW YORK

• • •

"When men make gods, there is no God!"
—EUGENE O'NEILL

Frank McCourt:

"I admire certain priests and nuns who go off on their
own and do God's work on their own, who help in the ghettos,
but as far as the institution of the Church is concerned,
I think it is despicable."

"And, of course, they've always condemned dancing. You know, you might touch a member of the opposite sex. And you might get excited and you might do something natural."

"Religion promotes the divine discontent within oneself, so that one tries to make oneself a better person and draw oneself closer to God."
—CYRIL CUSACK, ACTOR

• • •

"Jesus is just a word I use to swear with."
—RICHARD HARRIS, ACTOR

• • •

"I think there's a bit of the devil in everybody. There's a bit of a priest in everybody, too, but I enjoyed playing the devil more. He was more fun."
—GABRIEL BYRNE, ACTOR

• • •

"Had you English not persecuted the Catholics in Ireland…the greatest number of them would before now have become Protestants."
—NAPOLEON BONAPARTE

Maureen O'Hara, actress:

"I have never lost my faith in God."

"I'm terrified about the day that I enter the gates of heaven and God says to me, 'just a minute.'"

"God has a most wicked sense of humor."

"I know that I'm going to Hell…and I think I might see
a few of you there!"
—KATHY GRIFFIN

4

The "Irish Question"

Ireland is "the Empire's ailing child."
—Winston S. Churchill

• • •

The "Irish Question" has existed since 1800 when the Act of Union united the Irish and British parliaments into one, meeting at Westminster. In truth Churchill's "ailing child" was an abused child, stripped of its language, its religious freedom, its right to nationhood. Ireland was mainly looked at as an economic pillar for the Empire, unfortunately populated by the Irish. In the span of a decade the British almost found a solution. Today it is known as the "Great Famine," a potato blight that wreaked havoc on the indigent Irish population. Estimates vary, but it has been gauged that the population of the island in 1840 was eight million souls. By 1850 the population had shrunk to four million. It is believed that

*two million died and another two million fled the island in coffin
ships to find refuge around the world, mostly in the
United States of America. Following the American Civil War many
of these refugees returned home as members of the Irish Republican
Brotherhood (IRB), determined to ferment revolution. They were
known as the "Fenians," followers of the ancient warrior of Irish
mythology, Fionn. But the Rising of '67 ended in disaster. The
British were adamant—Ireland would remain part of the
British Empire forever. In 1882 another generation of Fenians,
known as the "Invincibles," started a campaign of terror against the
British, but were thwarted by informers. The British had their
"Irish Question," but the Irish also discovered that they had their
"British Question"—which would not be militarily confronted
again until Easter 1916.*

• • •

"A dense population, in extreme distress, inhabit an island where
there is an Established Church, which is not their Church, and a
territorial aristocracy the richest of whom live in foreign capitals.
Thus you have a starving population, an absentee aristocracy, and
an alien Church—and in addition the weakest executive in the
world. That is the Irish Question."
—BENJAMIN DISRAELI, 1844

• • •

"Ulster will fight, and Ulster will be right."
—LORD RANDOLPH CHURCHILL (WINSTON'S FATHER)

• • •

"…[U]pon all of these Cromwell's record was a lasting bane. By an uncompleted process of terror, by an iniquitous land settlement, by the virtual proscription of the Catholic religion, by the bloody deeds already described, he cut new gulfs between the nations and the creeds. 'Hell or Connaught' were the terms he thrust upon the native inhabitants, and they for their part, across three hundred years, have used as their keenest expression of hatred 'The Curse of Cromwell on you.' …Upon all of us there still lies 'the curse of Cromwell.'"

—Winston S. Churchill

Oliver Cromwell:

"To hell or to Connaught."—As he dispersed the Catholics from their land and drove them to the west of Ireland in the 17th century

"I shall not, where I have the power…suffer the exercise of the Mass."

"[T]he righteous judgment of God on these barbarous wretches, who have imbued their hands with so much innocent blood."
—After the sacking of Catholic Drogheda

"Hang harpers, wherever found, and destroy their instruments."
—QUEEN ELIZABETH 1

• • •

During the Great Famine, Frederick Douglass, an
Afro-American abolitionist, was shocked by what he witnessed,
seeing families with nothing but "a board on a box for a table, rags
on straw for a bed, and a picture of the crucifixion on the wall."

"Families, when all was eaten and no hope left, took their last
look at the sun, built up their cottage doors that none might see
them die nor hear their groans, and were found weeks afterwards,
skeletons on their own hearth."
—JOHN MITCHEL, YOUNG IRELANDER, DESCRIBING
THE IRISH FAMINE IN HIS JAIL JOURNAL

But this Irish crucifixion seemed to be just what the Lord ordered,
according to Sir Charles Trevelyan, the man in charge of famine
relief in Ireland:

"The judgment of God sent the calamity to teach the Irish a
lesson, that calamity must not be too much mitigated… The real
evil with which we have to contend is not the physical evil of the
Famine, but the moral evil of the selfish, perverse, and turbulent
character of the people." He went on to describe the famine as

"a direct stroke of an all-wise and all-merciful Providence," one which laid bare "the deep and inveterate root of social evil." The famine, he declared, was "the sharp but effectual remedy by which the cure is likely to be effected… God grant that the generation to which this great opportunity has been offered may rightly perform its part…"

Michael Collins, as Minister for Finance in the first Dáil, was responsible for raising a National Loan to finance the inchoate Irish Republic. The British went on a systematic manhunt for the funds, sending bank examiners to Dublin go over the books of banks where they suspected Collins was hiding his money. This alarmed Collins to such an extent that he sent his personal assassination squad, "The Twelve Apostles," to shoot one of the bank examiners, Alan Bell. The killing had the desired effect as no more bank examiners could be recruited by the British to go to Dublin. Winston Churchill, who would later become friends with Collins, took to tirade:

"Really getting very serious… What a diabolical streak [the Irish] have in their character! I expect it is that treacherous, assassinating, conspiring trait which has done them in in bygone ages of history and prevented them from being a great responsible nation with stability and prosperity. It is shocking that we have not been able to bring the murderers to justice."

"To all those who have suffered as a consequence of our troubled past I extend my sincere thoughts and deep sympathy. With the benefit of historical hindsight we can all see things which we would wish had been done differently or not at all."
—QUEEN ELIZABETH II ON HER STATE VISIT TO THE REPUBLIC OF IRELAND, DUBLIN CASTLE, MAY 2011

5

Revolution: The Irish Confront Their "British Question"

"Those who make peaceful revolution impossible will make violent revolution inevitable."
—JOHN F. KENNEDY

• • •

"Strum, strum and be hanged."
—THEOBALD WOLFE TONE TO A GATHERING OF HARPISTS, 1792

• • •

Sometimes it looks like the Irish may have invented revolution. And after her people, it may be Ireland's most important export.

The Irish have fought the good fight not only in their own country, but have transplanted it throughout the world. In Chile, Bernardo

O'Higgins is the national hero. In Cuba and South America, there is the legend of Che Guevara, a descendent of the Lynches of County Galway. In Mexico, the people still remember the heroes of the Batallón de San Patricio—*the St. Patrick's Battalion— members of the United States Army, many of them refugees from the Irish famine, who deserted the U.S. to join their fellow Mexican Catholics during the Mexican-American War. It is even rumored that the infamous Mexican highwayman, "Zorro," was based on one William Lamport, an Irish-Catholic adventurer. The Irish Republican Brotherhood was founded in New York City in 1859. And people forget that these "Fenians" twice invaded Canada from the U.S. in an attempt to "liberate" it from British hegemony.*

The names of revolutionaries who "stayed at home" to fight are legendary: Michael Collins, Eamon de Valera, Padraig Pearse, Jeremiah O'Donovan Rossa, Robert Emmet, Lord Edward Fitzgerald, to name just a few. Their words, both at home and abroad, still reverberate with threat, belligerence, hatred of oppression, love of liberty and, ultimately, hope for the future and the betterment of mankind.

Charles Stewart Parnell was called "The Uncrowned King of Ireland." As leader of the Irish Parliamentary Party he fought for "Home Rule" for Ireland. He was also a leader of the militant Land League. He was betrayed by his own party members and the Catholic Church—he was Protestant—over his affair with a married woman, Kitty O'Shea. (See James Joyce's take on the fall

of Parnell in A Portrait of the Artist as a Young Man *and also in "Ivy Day in the Committee Room" from* Dubliners.*) Parnell died on October 6, 1891 at the age of 45. The cause of death was said to be a broken heart.*

"No man has the right to fix the boundary to the march of a nation."

"When we have undermined English misgovernment, we have paved the way for Ireland to take her place amongst the nations of the earth. And let us not forget that that is the ultimate goal at which all we Irishmen aim. None of us, whether we be in America or in Ireland…will be satisfied until we have destroyed the last link which keeps Ireland bound to England."

"Ireland is not a geographical fragment of England; she is a nation."

Padraig Pearse was born on Great Brunswick (now Pearse) Street in Dublin in 1878. He was a lawyer, teacher and, ultimately, a revolutionary, holding the rank of Commandant-General. His was the "voice" of the revolution. He wrote Poblacht Na H Eireann, *the Irish Declaration of Independence that declared the Irish Republic on Easter Monday 1916. Under his command the General Post Office in Dublin held out for five days before surrendering. He was executed on May 3, 1916, by a British firing squad at Kilmainham Gaol.*

"There is only one way to appease a ghost. You must do the thing it asks you. The ghosts of a nation sometimes ask very big things and they must be appeased, whatever the cost."
—CHRISTMAS DAY 1915

"As long as Ireland is unfree the only honourable attitude for Irish men/women to have is an attitude of rebellion."

"Firing squads don't have reunions!"
—SEÁN LEMASS, FORMER *TAOISEACH* (PRIME MINISTER) OF IRELAND, ON WHY HE NEVER MENTIONED HIS PARTICIPATION IN THE ASSASSINATION OF THE BRITISH SECRET SERVICE ON BLOODY SUNDAY, NOVEMBER 21, 1920

• • •

"I put the two of them up against the wall. May the Lord have mercy on your souls. I plugged the two of them."
—Vincent Byrne, shooter, Michael Collins' Squad, the Twelve Apostles, on the events of Bloody Sunday, 1920

• • •

"Lads! Live with honor, or die with glory!
He who is brave, follow me!"
—Bernardo O'Higgins at the Battle of El Roble, 1813

• • •

"The first thing to note is that in my son's veins flowed the blood of the Irish rebels."
—Che Guevara's father commenting on his son

• • •

"We have no right to believe that freedom can be won without struggle."
—Che Guevara

• • •

"I spent a great deal of time with Che Guevara while I was in Havana. I believe he was far less a mercenary than he was a freedom fighter."
—Maureen O'Hara

*One of the "weapons" Irish revolutionaries used in the 20th century
was the hunger strike. The first rebel to shock the world with his
steadfastness was Terence MacSwiney (1879–1920), the
Lord Mayor of Cork. He starved to death at Brixton Prison in
England on October 25, 1920, after a fast of 74 days.*

"It is not those who can inflict the most, but those that can suffer
the most who will conquer."

"I am confident that my death will do more to smash the
British Empire than my release."

"I want you to bear witness that I die as a Soldier of the
Irish Republic."
<small>MacSwiney's last words to a visiting priest</small>

*Sixty-one years later Bobby Sands (1954–1981), a nationalist MP and
member of the Provisional IRA in Northern Ireland, died in the Maze
Prison near Belfast on May 5, 1981, after 66 days on hunger strike.
That day British Prime Minister Margaret Thatcher—proving she
never heard the lament of George Santayana that "Those who cannot
remember the past are condemned to repeat it"—said in the House of
Commons: "Mr. Sands was a convicted criminal. He chose to take his
own life. It was a choice that his organization [the IRA] did not allow
to many of its victims." Sands' death proved a boon to the recruitment
for the IRA, and to this day he remains an inspiration to many
insurgents throughout the world—including President Nelson Mandela
of South Africa who knows something about prison life.*

"Our revenge will be the laughter of our children."

"They have nothing in their whole imperial arsenal that
can break the spirit of one Irishman who doesn't want
to be broken."

"They won't break me because the desire for freedom, and the
freedom of the Irish people, is in my heart. The day will dawn
when all the people of Ireland will have the desire for freedom to
show. It is then that we will see the rising of the moon."

"If I die, God will understand. Tell everyone I'll see them
somewhere, sometime."

"My father was an open partisan of the Irish cause.
When Irish prisoners went on a hunger strike, he pleaded
with them to cease endangering their lives. In many circles
in Ireland, our family name is still associated with those
who fought for liberty."
—CHAIM HERZOG, PRESIDENT OF ISRAEL

• • •

"The Fenian is the artist in Irish politics.
He is an inspiration, an ornament, a hero."
—LIAM O'FLAHERTY, *THE LIFE OF TIM HEALY*

• • •

"Burn everything English but their coal."
—19ᵀᴴ CENTURY FENIAN BATTLE CRY

• • •

"The English possessed as many words for stealing as the
Irish had for seaweed or guilt."
—JOSEPH O'CONNOR, NOVELIST

• • •

"I am ready to die for Ireland, but I will not kill for Ireland."
—FRANCIS SHEEHY-SKEFFINGTON, PACIFIST MURDERED BY
CAPTAIN J.C. BOWEN-COLTHURST, 3ᴿᴰ BATTALION ROYAL
IRISH RIFLES, PORTOBELLO BARRACKS, 26 APRIL 1916

• • •

"Comfort the afflicted, afflict the comfortable."
—FINLEY PETER DUNNE, HUMORIST
AND WRITER FROM CHICAGO

• • •

British Tory in the House of Commons: "The sun never
sets on the British Empire!" "That's because God
wouldn't trust them in the dark!"
—TIM HEALY, MP, IRISH PARLIAMENTARY PARTY

• • •

"I have nothing to regret, to retract or take back…
I can only say: God Save Ireland!"
—EDWARD O'MEAGHER CONDON, FENIAN, 1867

• • •

"The republic stands for truth and honour. For all that is noblest in our race. By truth and honour, principle and sacrifice alone will Ireland be free."
—LIAM MELLOWS, IRA COMMANDANT-GENERAL

• • •

"If liberty is not entire it is not liberty."
—EAMON DEVALERA

• • •

"You British plundered half the world for your own profit. Let's not pass it off as the Age of Enlightenment."
—SIDNEY AARON "PADDY" CHAYEFSKY, AMERICAN WRITER AND HONORARY IRISHMAN

• • •

"No person knows better than you do that the domination of England is the sole and blighting curse of this country. It is the incubus that sits on our energies, stops the pulsation of the nation's heart, and leaves to Ireland not gay vitality but horrid the convulsions of a troubled dream."
—DANIEL O'CONNELL IN AN 1831 LETTER TO BISHOP DOYLE

• • •

O Paddy dear, and did you hear the news that's going round?
The shamrock is forbid by law to grow on Irish ground;
St. Patrick's Day no more we'll keep, his colours can't be seen,
For there's a bloody law against the wearing of the green.
—DION BOUICAULT, ACTOR AND PLAYWRIGHT

• • •

PARAS THIRTEEN
BOGSIDE NIL
—DERRY GRAFFITI AFTER BLOODY SUNDAY 1972,
WHEN THE BRITISH ARMY MURDERED 13 UNARMED CIVILIANS

James Larkin, labor agitator:

"The land of Ireland for the people of Ireland."

"No, men and women of the Irish race, we shall not fight for England. We shall fight for the destruction of the British Empire and the construction of an Irish republic."

"Stop at home. Arm for Ireland. Fight for Ireland and no other land."

"We shall not fight for the preservation of the enemy, which has laid waste with death and desolation the fields and hills of Ireland for 700 years."

"Hell is not hot enough, nor eternity long enough, to punish these miscreants."
—BISHOP DAVID MORIARTY OF KERRY IN REACTION TO THE FENIAN UPRISING OF 1867, SAFELY TAKING THE BRITISH SIDE

• • •

James Connolly, labor agitator and organizer and head of the Irish Citizen Army, executed May 12, 1916, by firing squad:

"If you strike at, imprison, or kill us, out of our prisons or graves we will still evoke a spirit that will thwart you,

and perhaps, raise a force that will destroy you! We defy you!
Do your worst!"

"We believe in constitutional action in normal times; we believe
in revolutionary action in exceptional times."

"The British government has no right in Ireland, never had any
right in Ireland, never can have any right in Ireland."

"Apostles of Freedom are ever idolised when dead,
but crucified when alive."

"When I came back to Dublin I was court-martialed [by the IRA]
in my absence and sentenced to death in my absence, so I said
they could shoot me in my absence."
—BRENDAN BEHAN

• • •

"A man can't be too careful in the choice of his enemies."
—OSCAR WILDE

• • •

"The complete normalization of the relationships within Ireland
and between Ireland and Britain can only be fully achieved by
ending partition and reuniting our people and the country."
—GERRY ADAMS

• • •

"Never confuse a single defeat with a final defeat."
—F. SCOTT FITZGERALD

The Irish forgive their great men when they are safely buried.
—IRISH SAYING

*Edmund Burke, the "Guardian" of the gate at Trinity College, also
had opinions on rebellion:*

"People crushed by laws have no hope but to evade power.
If the laws are their enemies, they will be enemies to the law;
and those who have most to hope and nothing to lose will
always be dangerous."

"In a democracy, the majority of the citizens is capable of exercising the most cruel oppressions upon the minority."

"Our patience will achieve more than our force."

"Bad laws are the worst sort of tyranny."

"Tyrants seldom want pretexts."

"I venture to say no war can be long carried on against the will of the people."

6

From the Dock: "Let No Man Write My Epitaph"

"We seem to have lost. We have not lost. To refuse to fight would have been to lose; to fight is to win. We have kept faith with the past and handed on a tradition to the future."
—Padraig Pearse

• • •

One of the "advantages" of the British judiciary system is that the accused gets to have his say from the dock. Irish patriots for over two hundred years have taken advantage of this "courtesy" and by doing so have, long after their own deaths, continued to sway history's opinion in Ireland's favor.

The United Irishmen were the instigators of the Rising of 1798. It was Ireland's first "modern" revolution and it was led by the gentry of the educated Protestant class:

"From my tenderest youth I have considered the union of Ireland with Great Britain as the scourge of the Irish nation. And that the people of this country can have neither happiness nor freedom whilst that connection endures. Every day's experience and every fact that arose convinced me of this truth; and I resolved, if I could, to separate the two countries. But as I knew Ireland could not of herself throw off the yoke, I sought for help wherever I could find it."
—THEOBALD WOLFE TONE, 10 NOVEMBER 1798

• • •

ROBERT EMMET.

"Let no man write my epitaph; for as no man who knows
my motives dare now vindicate them, let no prejudice or
ignorance asperse them… When my country takes her place
among the nations of the earth, then, and not till then, let my
epitaph be written."
—ROBERT EMMET, 19 SEPTEMBER 1803

• • •

*In 1798 Lord Edward FitzGerald died from wounds before
he could be brought to trial. His sister, Lady Lucy FitzGerald,
spoke for him:*

"Irishmen, Countrymen, it is Edward FitzGerald's sister who
addresses you; it is a woman but that woman is his sister; she
would therefore die for you as he did. I don't mean to remind

61

you of what he did for you. 'Twas no more than his duty. Without ambition he resigned every blessing this world could afford to be of use to you, to his Countrymen whom he loved better than himself, but in this he did no more than his duty; he was a Paddy and no more; he desired no other title than this."

The Patriots of 1916:

"Ireland has seen her sons—aye, and her daughters too!—suffer from generation to generation, always for the same cause, meeting the same fate, and always at the hands of the same power. Still, always a fresh generation has passed on to withstand the same opposition . . . the Unionist champions chose a path which they felt would lead to the woolsack, while I went down the road I knew must lead to the dock, and the event proved we were both right."
—ROGER CASEMENT, AT HIS TRIAL FOR TREASON, LONDON, JUNE 30, 1916

• • •

Roger Casement was the only 1916 leader to have a show trial in London and get a chance to speak from the dock. He was hanged at Pentonville Prison, London, 3 August 1916.

The rebels surrendered on Saturday, 29 April 1916, and the British were in a terrible rush. Between 3 May and 12 May, fifteen leaders were executed by firing squad. They did not stand in a dock, but they left us these words of resistance and defiance:

"They think they have pacified Ireland. They think that they have purchased half of us and intimidated the other half. They think they have foreseen everything, think that they provided against everything; but the fools, the fools, the fools!—they have left us our Fenian dead, and while Ireland holds these graves, Ireland unfree shall never be at peace."
—Padraig Pearse, funeral oration for
Jeremiah O'Donovan Rossa, Glasnevin Cemetery,
1 August 1915

• • •

"When I was a child of ten, I went on my bare knees by my bedside one night and promised God that I should devote my life to an effort to free my country. I have kept the promise.
I have helped to organise, to train, and to discipline my fellow countrymen to the sole end that, when the time came, they might fight for Irish freedom . . . If you strike us down now, we shall rise again and renew the fight. You cannot conquer Ireland; you cannot extinguish the Irish passion for freedom. If our deed has not been sufficient to win freedom, then our children will win it by a better deed."
—Padraig Pearse, Commandant-General,
at court-martial on day the before his
execution at Kilmainham Gaol, 2 May 1916

• • •

"I and my fellow signatories believe we have struck the first successful blow for Irish freedom. The next blow, which we have no doubt Ireland will strike, will win through. In this belief, we die happy."
—Tom Clarke, executed Kilmainham Gaol, 3 May 1916. Clarke was a naturalized American citizen but kept it a secret because he wanted to be executed. Sacrifice for Ireland was more important to Clarke than his life

• • •

"We bleed that the nation may live. I die that the nation may live. Damn your concessions, England; we want our country." Before his execution, MacDiarmada wrote, "I feel happiness the like of which I have never experienced. I die that the Irish nation might live!"
—Seán MacDiarmada, executed Kilmainham Gaol, 12 May 1916

• • •

James Connolly, Commandant-General, Dublin Division, Army of the Irish Republic, 9 May 1916. Executed—sitting in a chair because of wounds—Kilmainham Gaol, 12 May 1916:

"We went out to break the connection between this country and the British Empire and to establish an Irish Republic. We believed that the call we then issued to the people of Ireland was a nobler call, in a holier cause, than any call issued to them during this war, having any connection with the war. We succeeded in proving that Irishmen are ready to die endeavouring to win for Ireland those national rights which the British Government has been asking them to die to win for Belgium. As long as that remains the case, the cause of Irish freedom is safe."

"Believing that the British Government has no right in Ireland, never had any right in Ireland, and never can have any right in Ireland, the presence, in any one generation of Irishmen, of even a respectable minority, ready to die to affirm that truth, makes that Government forever a usurpation and a crime against human progress."

"I personally thank God that I have lived to see the day when thousands of Irish men and boys, and hundreds of Irish women and girls, were ready to affirm that truth and to attest it with their lives if need be."

The Legend of Kevin Barry's Ordeal

Kevin Barry was an 18-year-old medical student and a member of the IRA. In October 1920 he was apprehended by the British army while participating in an ambush near Church Street in Dublin. He was brought to Mountjoy Gaol and interrogated by the British. He smuggled this account out:

"He tried to persuade me to give the names, and I persisted in refusing. He then sent the sergeant out of the room for a bayonet. When it was brought in the sergeant was ordered by the same officer to point the bayonet at my stomach… The sergeant then said that he would run the bayonet into me if I did not tell…

The same officer then said to me that if I persisted in my attitude he would turn me out to the men in the barrack square, and he supposed I knew what that meant with the men in their present temper. I said nothing. He ordered the sergeants to put me face down on the floor and twist my arm… When I lay on the floor, one of the sergeants knelt on my back, the other two placed one foot each on my back and left shoulder, and the man who knelt on me twisted my right arm, holding it by the wrist with one hand, while he held my hair with the other to pull back my head. The arm was twisted from the elbow joint.

This continued, to the best of my judgment,
for five minutes. It was very painful… I still persisted in
refusing to answer these questions… A civilian came in and
repeated the questions with the same result. He informed me that
if I gave all the information I knew I could get off."

He was brought before a court martial by the British, but
remained defiant: "As a soldier of the Irish Republic, I refuse to
recognise the court." Michael Collins tried to break him out but
could not. His last words were: "It is nothing, to give one's life for
Ireland. I'm not the first, and maybe I won't be the last. What's
my life compared with the cause?" He was hanged in Mountjoy
Gaol on All Saints Day, November 1, 1920.

7

Michael Collins: "The Big Fellow" Evens the Odds

"You will not get anything from the British government unless you approach them with a bullock's tail in one hand and a landlord's head in the other."
—MICHAEL COLLINS

• • •

Michael Collins was born in County Cork on October 16, 1890. He was a Commandant-General in the IRA, head of the Irish Republican Brotherhood, and Minister for Finance in the First Dáil, responsible for raising the National Loan that financed the infant nation. Collins knew that every Irish revolutionary movement had been betrayed by informers and the superior intelligence network of the British government.

He became the Director of Intelligence of the IRA, and it was in this position that he systematically identified and traced every British agent in Dublin. He then organized his infamous assassination Squad, who soon nicknamed themselves "The Twelve Apostles."

On the morning of 21 November 1920—which became known as "Bloody Sunday" in the annals of Irish history—the Squad struck and assassinated fourteen Secret Service agents of the Crown. The message was heard loud and clear in London. A little over a year later, on 6 December 1921, Collins signed the Treaty at #10 Downing Street which created the modern Irish State.

"I rejoice in his memory, and will not be so disloyal to it as to snivel over his valiant death. So tear up your mourning and hang up your brightest colours in his honour; and let us all praise God that he did not die in a snuffy bed of a trumpery cough, weakened by age, and saddened by the disappointments that would have attended his work had he lived."
—GEORGE BERNARD SHAW TO COLLINS' SISTER THREE DAYS AFTER HIS DEATH

• • •

"He comes from a brainy Cork Family."
—FIRST LINE OF A BRITISH POLICE DOSSIER ON MICHAEL COLLINS, DISCOVERED BY COLLINS HIMSELF DURING A "FACT FINDING" MISSION TO THE DUBLIN METROPOLITAN POLICE STATION, GREAT BRUNSWICK STREET, DUBLIN

• • •

"There is no crime in detecting and destroying in war-time, the spy and the informer. They have destroyed without trial. I have paid them back in their own coin."
—COLLINS COMMENTING ON THE EVENTS OF BLOODY SUNDAY

• • •

"They have died nobly at the hands of the firing squads. So much I grant. But I do not think the Rising week was an appropriate time for the issue of memoranda couched in poetic phrases, nor of actions worked out in a similar fashion. Looking at it from the inside (I was in the GPO) it had the air of a Greek tragedy about it, the illusion being more or less completed with the issue of the before mentioned memoranda. Of Pearse and Connolly I admire the latter the most. Connolly was a realist, Pearse the direct opposite. There was an air of earthy directness about Connolly. It impressed me. I would have followed him through hell had such action been necessary. But I honestly doubt very much if I would have followed Pearse—not without some thought anyway."

—ON THE EASTER RISING AND PEARSE AND CONNOLLY

• • •

"Lloyd George's attitude I find to be particularly obnoxious. He is all comradely—all craft and wiliness—all arm around the shoulder—all the old friends act… Not long ago he would joyfully have had me at the rope end. He thinks that the past is all washed out now—but that's to my face. What he thinks behind my back makes me sick at the thought of it."

—ON THE BRITISH PRIME MINISTER

• • •

"Give us the future… We've had enough of your past… Give us back our country…to live in—to grow in—to love."

"To me the task is a loathsome one. I go, I go in the spirit of a soldier who acts against his best judgment at the orders of his superior."

—ON BEING SENT TO THE TREATY NEGOTIATIONS BY DE VALERA

• • •

"To go for a drink is one thing. To be driven to it is another."

—ON THE FRUSTRATIONS OF THE TREATY NEGOTIATIONS

• • •

"Think—what have I got for Ireland? Something which she has wanted these past 700 years. Will anyone be satisfied with the bargain? Will anyone? I tell you this—early this morning I signed my own death warrant. I thought at the time how odd, how ridiculous—a bullet might just as well have done the job five years ago."
—AFTER SIGNING THE TREATY, 6 DECEMBER 1921

• • •

"In my opinion it gives us freedom, not the ultimate freedom that all nations desire…but the freedom to achieve it."
—DEFENDING THE TREATY DURING THE DEBATES

• • •

"Yerra, they'll never shoot me in my own county."
—JUST BEFORE LEAVING TO MEET HIS FATE AT BÉAL NA MBLÁTH

• • •

"Deputies have spoken about whether dead men would approve of it, and they have spoken whether children yet unborn would approve it, but few have spoken of whether the living approve it."
—DURING THE TREATY DEBATES

• • •

"Michael Collins rose looking as though he were going to shoot someone, preferably himself. In all my life I have never seen so much pain and suffering in restraint."
—CHURCHILL ON COLLINS AFTER THE SIGNING OF THE TREATY

• • •

Michael Collins: "The Big Fellow" Evens the Odds

"I shall not last long; my life is forfeit, but I shall do my best.
After I am gone it will be easier for others."
—COLLINS TO WINSTON CHURCHILL AT THEIR LAST MEETING

• • •

"He was an Irish patriot, true and fearless… When in future
times the Irish Free State is not only prosperous and happy,
but an active and annealing force…regard will be paid by
widening circles to his life and to his death… Successor to a
sinister inheritance, reared among fierce conditions and moving
through ferocious times, he supplied those qualities of action and
personality without which the foundations of Irish nationhood
would not have been re-established."
—CHURCHILL ON COLLINS AFTER HIS ASSASSINATION

• • •

8

Ferocious Irish Women

"Dress suitably in short skirts and sitting boots, leave your jewels and gold wands in the bank, and buy a revolver."
— Countess Markievicz's advice to female rebels

• • •

In the summer of 1971 I went to visit my Aunt Kathleen McEvoy Bartley, the matriarch of the McEvoy family, at her humble abode in Phibsborough, Dublin. It was the first time I met her and she was a typical McEvoy, very pink, obviously a blonde in her youth, still radiant and beautiful in her 74th year. I knew of the heroes of 1916 and I asked her—in the wisdom of my 20 years—if the whole thing, this revolution thing, hadn't been blown out of proportion. Now my Aunt Kathleen was a daily communicant and the mother of both a priest and a nun, and she leaned forward in her kitchen chair—called her "throne" by the family—and told me of Easter

Ferocious Irish Women

Week 1916 in Dublin, and about the dairy she worked at in North King Street, not that far from the Four Courts where the rebels had seized control. She told me she saw a British soldier drag an innocent man into a shop doorway and shoot him dead. It was an event that had galvanized her life. I asked her what she did in response? She told me she joined the Cumann na mBan, *the women's auxiliary of the Irish Volunteers, which soon became the IRA. Her story is not atypical of the times.*

To say that Irish women are tough is a redundancy. Traditionally, through famine, male drunkenness, massive immigration, revolution, and having more babies than God ever intended, the Irish family has been held together by the woman, not the man. Going as far back as the Ladies Land League, run by Anna Parnell, sister of Charles Stewart Parnell, Irish women have influenced the politics and culture of Ireland.

In the early 20th century Inghinidhe na hÉireann, *(Daughters of Erin) was founded by Maud Gonne to bring young women—who had been totally ignored by such male-dominated groups as the Irish Republican Brotherhood—into the nationalistic fold. In 1913 the* Cumann na mBan *was formed to serve alongside the recently constituted Irish Volunteers. And it was through women like Maud Gonne, the Countess Markievicz and Kathleen Clarke that the revolutionary and political fate of Ireland was forged. Other legendary names include Grace Gifford Plunkett, widow of Joseph Plunkett; Dilly Dicker, Michael Collins' beautiful and spunky girlfriend from Mountjoy Street who dressed up as a man and stole top secret British documents for her boyfriend; novelist Dorothy Macardle, who did hard time in Kilmainham Gaol; Mrs. Terence MacSwiney, who became a staunch opponent of the Free State; Elizabeth O'Farrell, the GPO nurse who served as intermediary in the surrender of Padraig Pearse; and Mrs. Margaret Pearse, mother of Padraig and Willie, who later became a fierce opponent of the Treaty.*

It is believed that there were up to 200 Cumann na mBan *women involved in Easter Week, serving as cooks, nurses, couriers, and even sharpshooters. In fact,* Cumann na mBan *women were more militant than men like Michael Collins, voting 419 to 63 against ratification of the Treaty. Tough is too soft a word for these quixotic feminists.*

Maud Gonne MacBride was married to Seán MacBride (also executed in 1916) and was the long-time object of William Butler Yeats' romantic ambitions. She was active in many nationalistic and humanitarian endeavors throughout her life in Ireland. Her son, Seán MacBride, won the Nobel Peace Prize in 1974:

"The Famine Queen"— Gonne's sobriquet for Queen Victoria

"I have always hated war and am by nature and philosophy a pacifist, but it is the English who are forcing war on us, and the first principle of war is to kill the enemy."

"The English may batter us to pieces, but they will never succeed in breaking our spirit."

"I will go to no sanatorium in England, instead coming home and if put back in Holloway [Prison in England] shall hunger strike at once…what devils English officials are!"

Constance Gore-Booth was born in England (like Maud Gonne) in 1868. Her Anglo-Irish family had roots in County Sligo. After she married a Polish prince in 1900 she was known as the Countess Markievicz. She was bitten by the nationalist bug in the early 20th century and soon came under the influence of Maud Gonne and W.B. Yeats. She was a member of James Connolly's Irish Citizen Army and was second-in-command of St. Stephen's Green during Easter Week and initially sentenced to death (commuted to life imprisonment). She became the first woman elected—she was imprisoned at the time—to the British House of Commons in the election of 1918. She chose not to take her seat in Westminster, instead becoming a member of the First Dáil *in Dublin, serving as Minister for Labour:*

"I did what I thought was right and I stand by it."—At her court martial after the Easter Rising

"I do wish your lot had the decency to shoot me."
—On being told that her death sentence had been
commuted to life imprisonment

"I am a Republican, I won't say a die-hard, I say an undying
Republican, and to me, in that Treaty, you absolutely and
deliberately by swearing an oath to the King of England, put the
Republic behind you."—On the Treaty

"One thing she had in abundance—physical courage; with that
she was clothed as with a garment."
—SEAN O'CASEY ON THE COUNTESS MARKIEVICZ

*The physical and mental anguish of the survivors is often ignored.
Yes, there were sixteen executions in 1916, but it is sometimes
forgotten that both Kathleen Clarke and Grace Plunkett suffered
miscarriages. And Clarke suffered the anguish of not only having
her husband Tom executed, but also her brother, Commandant
Edward (Ned) Daly, who commanded the Four Courts during the
Rising. She would go on to become the first woman Lord Mayor
of Dublin. Her first act in office was to evict a portrait of
Queen Victoria from the Mansion House:*

"I pictured countless dangers for my children, and went from that
to my husband and all he had suffered during those terrible years
in prison. Memories of Kilmainham came alive, and from that
my mind went to the prison yard where I pictured him shot, not

dead, but wounded to death and left to die slowly, in agony, or else finished off by an officer with a pistol. A story had circulated after the Rising that one of the executed men had met with that fate, and I always feared it had been he."—On her imprisonment in Holloway Prison in England in 1918

"The rights accorded [to women] in the Proclamation were the result of the considered opinion, after lengthy deliberation, of the minds of seven men who, I have heard President de Valera say, were supermen. They were not intended as a mere gesture to be set aside when (or if) success crowned the fight for freedom."

Hanna Sheehy-Skeffington's husband, Francis, was murdered by the British during Easter Week:

"Mr. de Valera shows mawkish distrust of women which has always coloured his outlook; his was the only command in Easter Week where the help of women (of the *Cumann na mBan*, women's auxiliary to the Irish Volunteers) was refused. He sent the women home; some went to other areas and were welcomed, and de Valera, as I heard him say somewhat sheepishly years later, 'lost some good men who had to be cooks in their place'… Connolly, in his Citizen Army, would have welcomed women as soldiers were they so minded, and he saw to it long before that those that were, had military training…"

"I recognize no partition. I recognize it as no crime to
be in my own country. I would be ashamed of my own
name and my murdered husband's name if I did…
Long live the Republic!"—On being arrested for entering
Northern Ireland in 1933

• • •

"It has been said here on several occasions that Padraig Pearse
would have accepted this Treaty. I deny it. As his mother I deny it,
and on his account I will not accept it. Neither would his brother
Willie accept it, because his brother was part and parcel of him."
—MRS. MARGARET PEARSE

• • •

"The revolutionary men and women must insist that men and women in Ireland have equal rights and duties and a surrender of any one of those rights or duties is treason to Ireland."
—Nora Connolly O'Brien,
James Connolly's daughter

• • •

"I saw my husband in his cell for ten minutes. During the interview the cell was packed with officers and a sergeant, who kept a watch in his hand and closed the interview by saying 'Your ten minutes is now up.'"
—Grace Gifford Plunkett on her "honeymoon" meeting with her new husband, Joseph Mary Plunkett, shortly after their wedding and hours before he was executed at Kilmainham Gaol

• • •

"For the defeat of the Republicans was a victory for England, not for Ireland; the leaders who had achieved it had defeated their own cherished ends. They, too, had desired the Republic; they all agreed to the Treaty only for fear that refusal would bring another war on Ireland and, in consenting, had brought war on Ireland themselves. In this lay the tragic irony of their victory: they had accomplished for the English what the English might have failed to accomplish for themselves."
—Dorothy Macardle, author

• • •

"Far better the grave of a rebel without cross, without stone, without name than a treaty with treacherous England that can only bring sorrow and shame."
—BRIDIE HALPIN, PRISONER, KILMAINHAM GAOL

The "Troubles" in Northern Ireland in the latter part of the 20th century brought more Fenian women to the fore. One of these was Bernadette Devlin McAliskey, a socialist agitator, who was elected to the British Parliament in 1969. Her charismatic personality, for a while, became the face of an oppressed minority:

"To gain that which is worth having, it may be necessary to lose everything else."
—*THE PRICE OF MY SOUL*

"My function in life is not to be a politician in Parliament: it is to get something done."

"It wasn't long before people discovered the final horrors of letting an urchin into Parliament."

The sacrifice, intellectualism, and political savvy that were displayed by Irish women for over a hundred years finally found a living symbol when Mary Robinson was elected President of Ireland in 1990. Mrs. Robinson, a former Senator, was a well-known liberal agitator for women's rights—including the right to contraception—

in the Republic before her election. She became the first Irish President to meet with Queen Elizabeth II at Buckingham Palace. After her presidency she became the United Nations High Commissioner for Human Rights. She was succeeded as President by Mary McAleese of Belfast.

"I was elected by men and women of all parties and none, by many with great moral courage who stepped out from the faded flags of the Civil War and voted for a new Ireland. And above all by the women of Ireland—*Mna na hEireann*—who instead of rocking the cradle rocked the system and who came out massively to make their mark on the ballot paper and on a new Ireland."

"In a society where the rights and potential of women are constrained, no man can be truly free. He may have power, but he will not have freedom."

Edna O'Brien:

"The vote means nothing to women. We should be armed."

"I have some women friends but I prefer men. Don't trust women. There is a built-in competition between women."

"What pisses me off is when I've got seven or eight record company fat pig men sitting there telling me what to wear."
—SINEAD O'CONNOR

• • •

"Never, never listen to anybody that tries to discourage you."
—MARIAH CAREY

Maureen O'Hara:

"Above all else, deep in my soul, I'm a tough Irishwoman."

"I didn't let anyone push me into things I didn't want to do where my career was concerned. So why did I crumble when it came to men?"

"I'm afraid I'm not sufficiently inhibited about the things that other women are inhibited about for me. They feel that you've given away trade secrets."
—MARY MCCARTHY

Margaret Mitchell, author of Gone With the Wind:

"The usual masculine disillusionment is discovering that a woman has a brain."

"With enough courage, you can do without a reputation."

"Until you've lost your reputation, you never realize what a burden it was."

Mary Harris Jones—"Mother Jones"—was born in County Cork in 1837. By the turn of the 20th century she was called "the most dangerous woman in America." Her union organizing led to her being called "the grandmother of all agitators," on the floor of the U.S. Senate. She replied that "I hope to live long enough to be the great-grandmother of all agitators." She got her wish—she lived to be 93. Mother Jones *magazine is named in her honor.*

"I asked a man in prison once how he happened to be there and he said he had stolen a pair of shoes. I told him if he had stolen a railroad he would be a United States Senator."

"Pray for the dead and fight like hell for the living."

"I abide where there is a fight against wrong."

"The employment of children is doing more to fill prisons, insane asylums, almshouses, reformatories, slums, and gin shops than all the efforts of reformers are doing to improve society."

"Sit down and read. Educate yourself for the coming conflicts."

"You don't need the vote to raise hell!"

"No matter what the fight, don't be ladylike! God almighty made women, and the Rockefeller gang of thieves made the ladies."

9

The Orangemen Have Their Say: The World According to Ian Paisley

"I would rather be British than be fair!"
—Ian Paisley

• • •

Every story needs a villain. And the villain—as if sent from central casting—to the Catholics of Northern Ireland during the "Troubles" of the late 20th century was the Reverend Ian Paisley, the fundamentalist Protestant minister who was a foe of the Provisional IRA and friend and supporter to his fellow Orange paramilitary men. And just as the nationalists have their heroes in the likes of Pearse, Connolly and Plunkett, the Orangemen also have

their own: the Dublin-born Sir Edward Carson, the tormentor
of Oscar Wilde and the prosecutor of Sir Roger Casement
(21 years apart), and Sir James Craig, the first Prime Minister
of the Northern Ireland, famous for saying "All I boast of is that we
are a Protestant Parliament and a Protestant State." (Although
the statement is not that much different from Eamon de Valera's
view of the Republic as being a Catholic state, it was looked on
with horror by the minority Catholic population and, as history
would prove, with justification.) Paisley fits right into this strident
tradition. Paisley is part man of God, part politician, part
cheerleader, part bigot, part crazy uncle—and all gadfly.
His views on everything from politics to sex—albeit somewhat

colorful—are certainly out of another age. (In fact, his views on sex would be cheered by the Roman Catholic Church.) And it was to the amazement of almost everyone that he was to become an important player in the transition of Northern Ireland, in 2007 becoming the First Minister of the new Northern Irish Government (sharing power successfully with former IRA gunman Martin McGuinness). Take it away, Rev. Paisley…

"Save Ulster from Sodomy" *Paisley's slogan in his 1977 campaign to stop homosexuality from being decriminalized in Northern Ireland*

"Line dancing is as sinful as any other type of dancing, with its sexual gestures and touching. It is an incitement to lust."

"We are not prepared to stand idly by and be murdered in our beds."

"I will never sit down with Gerry Adams…he'd sit with anyone. He'd sit down with the devil. In fact, Adams does sit down with the devil."

"Come into my parlor, said the spider to the fly, it's the nicest wee parlor you ever did spy…well, let me tell you Charles J. Haughey, the Ulster people are too fly to come into your parlor." *Paisley dismissing* Taoiseach *Haughey's invitation for unionists to come into a united Ireland in 1980*

"He never let me down." Paisley praising *Taoiseach* Bertie Ahern for his role in the peace talks

"Today at long last we are starting upon the road—I emphasize starting—which I believe will take us to lasting peace in our Province… Today we salute Ulster's honored and unaging dead—the innocent victims, that gallant band, members of both religions, Protestant and Roman Catholic, strong in their allegiance to their differing political beliefs, Unionist and Nationalist, male and female, children and adults, all innocent victims of the terrible conflict… I have sensed a great sigh of relief amongst all our people who want the hostility to be replaced with neighborliness… I believe that Northern Ireland has come to a time of peace, a time when hate will no longer rule. How good it will be to be part of a wonderful healing in our Province."

10

Kitchen Table Philosophy: Putting an Ass on the Cat

I remember in the 1950s sitting at the dinner table at night. My father, a Greenwich Village "super" and plumber, would come home and immediately take his pants off and sit in his underwear. This confused me because Jim Anderson (Robert Young) of Father Knows Best *on the TV would always come home from work, take off his jacket and replace it with another jacket, which mystified me. He sure wasn't like my Daddy.*

Pretty soon my father (also named Dermot McEvoy) would discourse on the events of the day. His conversation was liberally endowed with the adages of his native County Louth where he worked the land. Some of his laconic gems remain in my head to this day:

"When God made time, He made plenty of it."
A woman was never naked, "She was in her nude."
On seeing an oddly mated couple: "As He made them, He matched them."
On being asked the cause of death: "The last breath left him."

Across the table from my father, my mother would take it all in then remind us that our father was only another one of her many "crosses to bear."

I've asked some friends in the writing trade if they remembered any kitchen table philosophies from their youth and have been rewarded:

Maureen Dowd, author and *New York Times* columnist:

My dad had a list of Gaelic sayings that included: "Never bolt the door with a boiled carrot." That works for all occasions. Also, "Every old sock meets an old shoe." And: "A sock with holes is better than no sock at all."

My mom used to say: "God bless the corpse that the rain falls on" and "Better to be hung for a sheep than a lamb." And "You've got your name and your thanks," which somehow means that you'd offer to do something you don't want to do and then don't have to but they know you've offered.

"The devil you know is better than the devil you don't know."

Mary Kenny, Irish feminist, journalist and columnist:

My mother's favourite was: "It would be a poor world if we were all the same." And I think that really is wise.

"Listen to the river, and you will catch the fish." I like that because it can be about being observant, and also being intuitive.

Another is: "It is for his own benefit that the cat purrs." It's said that Celtic culture likes nature references (that's why Patrick so wisely chose the shamrock to illustrate his Trinity theology!).

My aunt Nora, from County Galway, used to say: "When you're too good, you're no good." I can see the truth of this now as a carer to my invalid husband: if I wear myself out attending to an almighty range of chores, I end up being such a wet rag that I'm no good to anyone.

Another rather crabby reflection, again from my Ma: "Eaten bread is soon forgotten." Those you entertain may not always reciprocate…not always true, by any means. But it can be.

Peasant wisdom is often conservative—I think it comes from watching the seasons repeat over and over (and maybe human folly repeat over and over too!)

Not only conservative, but fatalistic: "You can't make a silk purse out of a sow's ear." I didn't like hearing that because I felt it damned people's talents and their potential. It went with: "Water seeks its own level"—people only rise to their capacities.

On the other hand, the Jesuit saying, often quoted in Ireland: "Give me the child until he is seven and I will give you the man" was originally a statement about the enlightenment of education. A good early formation will stick. Now it is often quoted as an example of brain-washing…

Some Irish sayings are skeptical of human nature, but some can be easygoing and tolerant: "Every cripple has his own way of walking" is a kindly Irish saying.

The nuns at our convent were fond of saying that "Birds of a feather flock together"—the troublesome girls would always seek one another out. And I read the other day some psychologist saying that we do indeed seek like-minded others as our pals…

"Little apples grow again"—a great favourite of my late brother, Carlos. It has something of the same meaning as "Revenge is a dish best served cold."

"The old dog for the hard road"—much quoted by old Dublin journos in my youth. You can always depend on the veteran to get the job done! The older I get, the more I like it!

Rosemary Mahoney, author, *Down the Nile*:

If you asked one of my mother's family to say a prayer for you, they would respond, "Sure, my prayers go no higher than the fish in Shandon!" meaning you were wasting your time asking them to appeal to God on your behalf as they had no special "in" with him and their prayers wouldn't reach him. It's a reference to the famous weathervane of a fish on the top of St. Anne's church in Shandon Street in Cork. (The bells of that church are the bells in the song "The Bells of Shandon" written by a relative of me own, Francis Sylvester Mahony.) The prayers would go no higher than that earthbound fish. That steeple, by the way, has four sides to it and each side bears a clock. But none of the clocks ever tells the same time as the others (except for some reason on the hour), so the steeple is known, excellently, as "The Four-Faced Liar." You probably already know that.

Speaking of Mahony, in the U.S. when they met a person named Connor or Mahoney or Donnelly or any one of the Irish names that properly had an O' before it back in Ireland, they would say, "Well, it used to be O'Connor, but they dropped the O in the ocean on the way over!"

If I saw my mother staring at me and said to her, "What are you looking at?" she would say, "A cat can look at a king!" Another thing she would say if we stayed up too late at night: "You'll be crying in the morning, red-eye!"

If my great-aunt liked a person she would say, "He's the nicest man that ever wore a hat."

Another one that I remember but don't know who it came from is this: "What the fox can't catch he calls rotten."

My mother's family also had a lot of code words attached to people they knew from their village in Limerick. So, if a person walking into the restaurant in Boston was fat, they would look at each other and say knowingly "Nar Brown." Apparently Nar Brown was the fattest person in their village. If they said to you "Christy Slattery" it meant that your fly was down. I guess Christy Slattery was a mentally deficient guy in their village who couldn't remember to zip up his fly. If a person got drunk they would say "He was Mary and Hanny." I don't know who Mary and Hanny were, but they must have been drunks!

Alphie McCourt, author, *A Long Stone's Throw:*

TB was rampant in the Fifties. A shameful disease. To have it, meant that you and your family were dirty. A neighbor died. "What did he die of?" I asked my mother. "He died out of his health" she said. Nice code.

On those rare occasions when she might have a small treat—a glass of cider, a piece of cake or a trip to the movies, she had to ward off the guilt. "We'll be a long time dead," was her mantra.

And, of course, one of the best: "Wasn't he a lovely corpse." Or, "I might as well be drunk as the way I am."

"Fools' names and fools' faces are often seen in public places—and more than once."

Peter Quinn, author, *Banished Children of Eve*:

One of my all-time favorite expressions is from one of my best friend's Kerry-born mother. She liked to say of skilled artisans (especially carpenters), "Ach, he could put an ass on a cat."

11

Love Irish Style: Sex, Romance & Marriage

"Between men and women there is no friendship possible. There is passion, enmity, worship, love, but no friendship."
—OSCAR WILDE

• • •

Carson McCullers once wrote a book with the most haunting and truthful title of all time. It was called The Heart Is A Lonely Hunter. *It reminds us that the most desperate need of any human being is to be loved, to be desired, to be treasured. The Irish, of course, are no exception. But to compound the problem, they are Irish. A race with the pagan needs of the Druids, the romance of ancient Celts, and the manufactured guilt complexes of the Catholic Church. Their poets, like Yeats, gave romance to love.*

Their writers, like Joyce, gave sex to love. And their Catholic clerics gave guilt to both love and sex. A race in full, mad pursuit of romance, but also a race of extraordinary spinsters and eternal bachelors. A race, like the rest of the world, entranced by love, but also frightened by its consequences.

"…I asked him with my eyes to ask again yes and then he asked me would I yes to say yes my mountain flower and first I put my arms around him yes and drew him down to me so he could feel my breasts all perfume yes and his heart was going like mad and yes I said yes I will Yes."
—MOLLY BLOOM'S SOLILOQUY, *ULYSSES*

• • •

As the old cock crows the young cock learns.
—IRISH SAYING

• • •

"As usual, there is a great woman behind every idiot."
—JOHN LENNON

Eavan Boland, poet:

"Love will heal
What language fails to know"

"He died in the Asylum in Mullingar. Of mental illness. Or drink.
Or that combination of both which in Ireland, as anywhere else,
might just cover a broken heart."
—FROM *OBJECT LESSONS*

"I am the least difficult of men. All I want is boundless love."
—FRANK O'HARA, POET

*James Stephens was born in Dublin in 1882 and is known for his
poems and retellings of Irish myths and fairy tales. He was a friend
of James Joyce and the author of* Crock of Gold. *His book,*

The Insurrection in Dublin, *is perhaps the best eyewitness account of the events of Easter Week 1916:*

"A woman is a branchy tree and man a singing wind; and from her branches carelessly he takes what he can find."

"Women and birds are able to see without turning their heads, and that is indeed a necessary provision for they are both surrounded by enemies."

"Men come of age at sixty, women at fifteen."

"What the heart knows today the head will understand tomorrow."

Nuala O'Faolain, novelist:

"I did believe, from my experience of life and of looking at the world, that men hated women."
—FROM *MY DREAM OF YOU*

"Lovers are allowed to be as cruel as anything to the one who disappoints them."
—FROM *MY DREAM OF YOU*

• • •

She sighed and she did swear that she never would deceive me

But the devil take the women for they never can be easy
—FROM "WHISKEY IN THE JAR"

Although Oscar Wilde is thought of as a gay icon, people forget that he was bisexual, married, and the father of two children. Oscar saw the battle of the sexes from a unique perspective:

"Keep love in your heart. A life without it is like a sunless garden when the flowers are dead."

"How can a woman be expected to be happy with a man who insists on treating her as if she were a perfectly normal human being."

"One should always be in love. That is the reason one should never marry."

"A man's face is his autobiography. A woman's face is her work of fiction."

"All women become like their mothers. That is their tragedy. No man does. That's his."

"Men always want to be a woman's first love—women like to be a man's last romance."

"I see when men love women. They give them but a little of their lives. But women when they love give everything."

"Bigamy is having one wife too many. Monogamy is the same."

"Hatred is blind, as well as love."

"Women are made to be loved, not understood."

"To love oneself is the beginning of a lifelong romance."

"Deceiving others. That is what the world calls a romance."

"Who, being loved, is poor?"

"Men marry because they are tired; women, because they are curious; both are disappointed."

"Woman begins by resisting a man's advances and ends by blocking his retreat."

"The world has grown suspicious of anything that looks like a happily married life."

"Romance should never begin with sentiment. It should begin with science and end with a settlement."

"No woman should ever be quite accurate about her age. It looks so calculating."

"There is nothing so difficult to marry as a large nose."

"In married life three is company and two none."

"To marry the Irish is to look for poverty."
—J.P. Donleavy

• • •

"The thing about love is that we come alive in
bodies not our own."
—Colum McCann, *Let the Great World Spin*

• • •

"Everything is clearer when you're in love."
—John Lennon

Bram Stoker, inventor of Dracula, *on the fairer sex:*

"I suppose that we women are such cowards that we think a man
will save us from fears, and we marry him."

"No man knows till he experiences it, what it is like to feel his
own life-blood drawn away into the woman he loves."

"Because if a woman's heart was free a man might have hope."

Two Hall of Fame baseball managers knew exactly what the battle of the sexes meant to their ballplayers:

"One percent of ballplayers are leaders of men. The other ninety-nine percent are followers of women."
—JOHN J. MCGRAW, MANAGER, NEW YORK GIANTS

• • •

"Being with a woman all night never hurt no professional baseball player. It's staying up all night looking for a woman that does him in."
—CHARLES DILLON (CASEY) STENGEL

P.J. O'Rourke is an Irish-American writer who often has a jaundiced view of life:

"There are a number of mechanical devices which increase sexual arousal, particularly in women. Chief among these is the Mercedes-Benz 380SL convertible."

"Never be unfaithful to a lover, except with your wife."

"There is one thing women can never take away from men. We die sooner."

And now a word from Errol Flynn, the man who gave us the immortal term: "In, like Flynn":

"The public has always expected me to be a playboy, and a decent chap never lets his public down."

"Women won't let me stay single and I won't let me stay married."

"I can't go too much into my domestic life because there are ex-wives ready to do me in."
—FRANK McCOURT

• • •

"Marriage is a custom brought about by women who then proceed to live off men and destroy them, completely enveloping the man in a destructive cocoon or eating him away like a poisonous fungus on a tree."
—RICHARD HARRIS

• • •

"But, you know, sex is controversial; it just is and it always will be."
—LIAM NEESON

James Joyce, the man who liked to write dirty books:

"Men are governed by lines of intellect—women: by curves of emotion."

"Love between man and man is impossible because there must not be sexual intercourse, and friendship between man and woman is impossible because there must be sexual intercourse."

• • •

"During the intervals the devil is busy; yes, very busy, as sad experience proves, and on the way home in the small hours of the morning, he is busier still."
—Irish Bishops' statement on all-night dances, 1933

Brendan Behan weighs in:

"The big difference between sex for money and sex for free is that sex for money usually costs a lot less."

"The most important things to do in the world are to get something to eat, something to drink, and somebody to love you."

• • •

"In every question and every remark tossed back and forth between lovers who have not played out the last fugue, there is one question and it is this: 'Is there someone new?'"
—Edna O'Brien

George Bernard Shaw:

"A broken heart is a very pleasant complaint for a man in London
if he has a comfortable income."

"Love is a gross exaggeration of the difference between
one person and everybody else."

"Every person carries in his heart the blueprint
of the one he loves."
—BISHOP FULTON J. SHEEN

• • •

"I used to go missing quite a lot... Miss Canada,
Miss United Kingdom, Miss World."
—GEORGE BEST, BELFAST-BORN WORLD CLASS FOOTBALLER

• • •

A man loves his sweetheart the most, his wife the best, but his
mother the longest.
—IRISH PROVERB

• • •

"How would you know a Cork footballer? He's the one who
thinks that oral sex is just talking about it."
—JOHN B. KEANE

• • •

Love Irish Style: Sex, Romance & Marriage

Irish foreplay: "Brace yerself, Brigid!"
—IRISH JOKE

• • •

"May you die in bed at ninety-five years,
shot by a jealous husband (or wife)."
—IRISH SAYING

Comedienne Rosie O'Donnell was one of the first stars to come out of the closet, declaring that she was a lesbian in 2002 and has been outspoken about LGBT issues:

"There are some heterosexuals that have heterosexual behavior that is appalling sexually, that is deviant and bad and not really moral and Christ-like and biblical. But those people are never questioned as to whether or not they're allowed to be a parent."

"I want the same standard applied to homosexuals
as is applied to heterosexuals."

"I think life is easier if you're straight."

"I've always enjoyed a woman's company more than men's.
They're usually better looking."
—HUGH LEONARD

Dublin-born Thomas Moore is famous for his song, "The Meeting of the Waters." Outside the front gate of Trinity College there stands a statue of Tommy Moore over what used to be a public lavatory. Leopold Bloom in Ulysses *comments as he walks by: "They did right to put him up over a urinal: meeting of the waters":*

"And the heart that is soonest awake to the flowers is always the first to be touch'd by the thorns."

"Romantic love is an illusion. Most of us discover this truth at the end of a love affair or else when the sweet emotions of love lead us into marriage and then turn down their flames."

"No, there's nothing half so sweet in life as love's young dream."

"Came but for friendship, and took away love."

"A pretty wife is something for the fastidious vanity of a rogue to retire upon."

"She danced a jig, she sung a song that took my heart away."
—WILLIAM ALLINGHAM

Oliver Goldsmith:

"Girls like to be played with, and rumpled a little too, sometimes."

"All that a husband or wife really wants is to be pitied a little, praised a little, and appreciated a little."

"Romance and novel paint beauty in colors more charming than nature, and describe a happiness that humans never taste. How deceptive and destructive are those pictures of consummate bliss!"

"When lovely woman stoops to folly, and finds too late that men betray, what charm can soothe her melancholy, what art can wash her guilt away?"

"They say women and music should never be dated."

"I chose my wife, as she did her wedding gown, for qualities that would wear well."

"You musn't force sex to do the work of love or love to do the work of sex."
—MARY MCCARTHY

• • •

"Some mistakes are too much fun to make only once."
—MARGARET MITCHELL

• • •

"I have a thing for red-haired Irish boys, as we know."
—SANDRA BULLOCK, ACTRESS

12

Once a Celtic Philosopher...

"Life is a solitary cell whose walls are mirrors."
—Eugene O'Neill

• • •

The French philosopher Voltaire was once invited to an orgy. He went and enjoyed himself. He was offered a second invitation, but declined, stating "Once a philosopher, twice a pervert." That's kind of how I feel about Celtic philosophers and philosophies. Some are brilliant, right-on and benefit from a divine touch. Some are not so brilliant, contradictory, bred on hopelessness, shifting snidely to the perverted side. Embrace or deride. You decide.

"More men die of jealousy than of cancer."
—Joseph P. Kennedy

One view, two different Irish angles:

"There are those who look at things the way they are, and ask why… I dream of things that never were, and ask why not?"
—ROBERT F. KENNEDY, QUOTING GEORGE BERNARD SHAW

• • •

"Some people see things that are and ask, Why? Some people dream of things that never were and ask, Why not? Some people have to go to work and don't have time for all that."
—GEORGE CARLIN

"Jealousy is the tribute mediocrity pays to genius."
—BISHOP FULTON J. SHEEN

• • •

Oh what a pleasant world 'twould be,
How easy we'd step thro' it,
If all the fools who meant no harm,
Could manage not to do it!
—FRANCIS LEDWIDGE

• • •

"What's the use of looking on the gloomy side of everything?"
— WILLIAM HENRY MCCARTHY, JR., AKA, BILLY THE KID

• • •

IS THERE LIFE *BEFORE* DEATH?
—BELFAST GRAFFITI DURING THE TROUBLES

• • •

"We are all in the gutter, but some of us are
looking at the stars."
—OSCAR WILDE, *LADY WINDERMERE'S FAN*

• • •

"Where I am, I don't know, I'll never know, in the silence you
don't know, you must go on, I can't go on, I'll go on."
—SAMUEL BECKETT, *THE UNNAMABLE*

• • •

"When you grow up on an island, what matters is
how you stand to the sea."
—RODDY DOYLE

• • •

"You just go on your nerve."
—FRANK O'HARA, POET

• • •

A good laugh and a long sleep are the best cures
in the doctor's book.
—IRISH PROVERB

• • •

"No fear, no jealousy, no meanness."
—LIAM CLANCY TO BOB DYLAN

• • •

"A man who is not afraid of the sea will soon be drowned…for he
will go out on a day he shouldn't. But we do be afraid of the sea,
and we only be drowned now and again."
—JOHN MILLINGTON SYNGE, *THE ARAN ISLANDS*

• • •

ESTRAGON: …Let's go.
VLADIMIR: We can't.
ESTRAGON: Why not?
VLADIMIR: We're waiting for Godot.
—SAMUEL BECKETT, *WAITING FOR GODOT*

• • •

Here's to a long life and a merry one
A quick death and an easy one
A pretty girl and an honest one
A cold beer and another one!
—IRISH TOAST

• • •

"I often looked up at the sky an' assed meself the question—what
is the moon, what is the stars?"
—SEAN O'CASEY, *JUNO AND THE PAYCOCK*

• • •

"Time you enjoy wasting was not wasted."
—JOHN LENNON

• • •

"I have a no-apology policy."
—KATHY GRIFFIN

• • •

"May you live all the days of your life."
—JONATHAN SWIFT

*There probably was no more tormented soul than American
arch-playwright Eugene O'Neill. He was born in a Times Square
hotel room on October 16, 1888, and went on to write plays about
tortured Irish soul including* Long Day's Journey Into Night,
The Iceman Cometh, *and* A Moon for the Misbegotten.

He won the Nobel Prize in Literature in 1936 and won the Pulitzer Prize four times:

"I am so far from being a pessimist...on the contrary, in spite of my scars, I am tickled to death at life."

"It's a great game—the pursuit of happiness."

"There is no present or future—only the past, happening over and over again—now."
—*A Moon for the Misbegotten*

• • •

"Man's loneliness is but his fear of life."

Once a Celtic Philosopher...

Oscar Wilde shares O'Neill's birthday, October 16th;
it is also the birthday of the revolutionary, Michael Collins.
As Oscar might warn, Beware of Irish Libras because those
scales of justice can be lethal:

"Always forgive your enemies—nothing annoys them so much."

"Education is an admirable thing, but it is well to remember
from time to time that nothing that is worth knowing can
be taught."

"The only way to get rid of temptation is to yield to it…
I can resist everything but temptation."

"True friends stab you in the front."

"Experience is simply the name we give our mistakes."

"There is only one thing in life worse than being talked about,
and that is not being talked about."

"There are only two tragedies in life: one is not getting what one
wants, and the other is getting it."

"When the gods wish to punish us they answer our prayers."

"Do you really think it is weakness that yields to temptation?
I tell you that there are terrible temptations which it requires
strength, strength, and courage to yield to."

"The truth is rarely pure and never simple."

"What is a cynic? A man who knows the price of everything and the value of nothing."

"Those whom the gods love grow young."

"There are only two kinds of people who are really fascinating—people who know absolutely everything, and people who know absolutely nothing."

"The basis of optimism is sheer terror."

"Pessimist: one who, when he has the choice of two evils, chooses both."

The Mets lose an awful lot?
Listen, mister. Think a little bit.
When was the last time you won anything out of life?
—JIMMY BRESLIN, ENDING, *CAN'T ANYBODY HERE PLAY THIS GAME?*

• • •

"Conviction without experience makes for harshness."
—FLANNERY O'CONNOR

• • •

"To say what you feel is to dig your own grave."
—SINEAD O'CONNOR

• • •

"No man knows till he has suffered from the night how sweet and dear to his heart and eye the morning can be."
—BRAM STOKER, *DRACULA*

• • •

"Irony is my constant companion."
—FRANK McCOURT

• • •

"From doing *A Moon for the Misbegotten*, I've learned that nobody's love can save anybody else. There are people who want to die, and nothing or nobody will stop them. The only one who can save you is yourself."
—GABRIEL BYRNE

• • •

"Make no judgments where you have no compassion."
—ANNE McCAFFREY, SCIENCE FICTION AND FANTASY AUTHOR

F. Scott Fitzgerald famously said "There are no second acts in American life," which is totally wrong. What he meant to say is that "I did not have a second act in my American life":

"Forgotten is forgiven."

"Life is essentially a cheat and its conditions are those of defeat; the redeeming things are not happiness and pleasure but the deeper satisfactions that come out of struggle."

"In a real dark night of the soul, it is always three o'clock in the morning, day after day."

"Glory is fleeting, but obscurity is forever."
—THOMAS MOORE

James Stephens:

"A sword, a spade, and a thought should never be allowed to rust."

"Curiosity will conquer fear even more than bravery will."

Once a Celtic Philosopher...

*George Bernard Shaw became the second Irishman to win the
Nobel Prize in Literature in 1925:*

"A life spent making mistakes is not only more honorable, but
more useful than a life spent doing nothing!"

"Martyrdom is the only way a man can become famous
without ability."

"The things most people want to know about are usually none of
their business."

Irish Sayings:

If you are looking for a friend without a fault, you will be without
a friend forever.

Neither give cherries to pigs nor advice to a fool.

He'd offer you an egg if you promised not to break the shell.

A silent mouth is sweet to hear.

An old broom knows the dirty corners best.

Edmund Burke:

"The only thing necessary for the triumph of evil is for good men to do nothing."

"By gnawing through a dike, even a rat may drown a nation."

"Sin has many tools, but a lie is the handle which fits them all."

"Toleration is good for all, or it is good for none."

"Never despair, but if you do, work on in despair."

"Facts are to the mind what food is to the body."

"If you can be well without health, you may be happy without virtue."

Oliver Goldsmith:

"Life is a journey that must be traveled no matter how bad the roads and accommodations."

"Every absurdity has a champion to defend it."

"Hope is such a bait; it covers any hook."

"Be not affronted at a joke. If one throw salt at thee, thou wilt receive no harm, unless thou art raw."

"Success consists of getting up just one more time than you fall."

"The company of fools may first make us smile, but in the end we always feel melancholy."

Mary McCarthy:

"People with bad consciences always fear the judgment of children."

"Every age has a keyhole to which its eye is pasted."

"In violence we forget who we are."

• • •

"I believe in the Corporal Works of Mercy, the Ten Commandments, the American Declaration of Independence, and James Connolly's outline of a socialist society… Most of my life I've been called a lunatic because I believe that I am my brother's keeper. I organize poor and exploited workers, I fight for the civil rights of minorities, and I believe in peace. It appears to have become old-fashioned to make social commitments—to want a world free of war, poverty, and disease. This is my religion."
—MICHAEL J. QUILL, EX-IRA MAN AND LEADER OF NEW YORK CITY'S TRANSPORT WORKERS UNION, WHO FAMOUSLY AND UNASHAMEDLY BROUGHT NEW YORK TO ITS KNEES WITH A TWO-WEEK TRANSIT STRIKE IN 1966

• • •

"So we beat on, boats against the current, borne back ceaselessly
into the past."
—F. Scott Fitzgerald, *The Great Gatsby*, last line

13

Writers & Poets

"Words are all we have."
—Samuel Beckett

• • •

Back in 1596 English poet Edmund Spenser wrote "A View of the Present State of Ireland." In it he stated that "Ireland is a diseased portion of the State, it must first be cured and reformed, before it could be in a position to appreciate the good sound laws and blessings of the nation." His solution? Destroy the natives' language, customs, and culture. A man two-and-a-half centuries ahead of his time, he thought famine might do the trick.

"One of the reasons the Irish have such a way with English is that they had no choice," says Irish-American author Rosemary Mahoney. "There was a time when the Irish were forbidden to speak their own language, forbidden to practice their religion, so the only thing left to them was to adopt the language of their oppressor. As you know, they more than succeeded in that." So, the English came to Ireland and took the Gaelic language away from the Irish. The Irish, in revenge, took the English language and turned it upside down, commandeering it as a form of rebellion against the English, proving that the pen was indeed mightier than the sword.

Over three hundred years later Spenser's threats were not forgotten.
Irish-American poet Marianne Moore wrote in "Spenser's Island":

It was Irish;
a match not a marriage was made
when my great great grandmother'd said
with native genius for
disunion, "Although your suitor be
perfection, one objection
is enough; he is not
Irish"…

The Irish say your trouble is their
trouble and your
joy their joy? I wish
I could believe it;
I am troubled, I'm dissatisfied, I'm Irish.

Probably the first Irish writer to turn his writing talent on the
British was Jonathan Swift, the Dean of St. Patrick's Cathedral
in Dublin. In 1729 he penned the perversely ironic A Modest
Proposal for Preventing the Children of Poor People From Being
a Burden to Their Parents or Country, and for Making Them
Beneficial to the Publick. *Known to all today simply as* A Modest
Proposal, *Swift went after the British for their exploitation of*
Ireland as an economic entity: "A young healthy child well nursed,
is, at a year old, a most delicious nourishing and wholesome food,
whether stewed, roasted, baked, or boiled; and I make no doubt
that it will equally serve in a fricassee, or a ragout…
I grant this food may be somewhat dear, and therefore very proper

for Landlords who, as they have already devoured most of the Parents, seem to have the best Title to the Children." Swift went on to conclude that "For this kind of commodity will not bear exportation, and flesh being of too tender a consistence, to admit a long continuance in salt, although perhaps I could name a country, which would be glad to eat up our whole nation without it."

Geez, I wonder what "country" Dean Swift could be thinking of?

No island nation on this planet has produced more great writers than Ireland. In the last century they have produced four Nobel Prize Winners in Literature: Yeats (1923), Shaw (1925), Beckett (1969), and Heaney (1995). And, of course, those laureates have a hell of a backup team, heavy with genius: O'Casey, Synge, Kavanagh, Swift, Kinsella, Ledwidge, Michael Longley, Edna Longley, Behan, Stoker, Flann O'Brien, Edna O'Brien, Roddy Doyle, Gogarty, Colum, Aogán Ó Rathaille, Wilde, Boland, Muldoon, Derek Mahon, Austin Clarke, Ní Dhomhnaill, Plunkett, Leonard, Medb McGuckian, Tóibín, Goldsmith, Dorothy Macardle, McCann, Joseph O'Connor, Frank O'Connor, Bowen, O'Flaherty, Stephens, and Lady Gregory.

And they are ably supported on the American side of the Atlantic by the likes of Eugene O'Neill, F. Scott Fitzgerald, John Gregory Dunne, Pete Hamill, Stewart O'Nan, Frank McCourt, Jimmy Breslin, Maeve Brennan, Rosemary Mahoney, Joseph Mitchell, Mary McCarthy, Peter Quinn, John O'Hara, Frank O'Hara, William Kennedy, Alice McDermott, Edwin O'Connor, Cormac McCarthy, Margaret Mitchell, Mary Higgins Clark, J.P. Donleavy, and Maureen Dowd.

Today it is ironic that Ireland has finally embraced all the writers she shunned in the years past, even those she censored—with the happy collaboration of the Catholic Church—by banning their books in the Irish state. In Dublin, opposite the General Post Office in O'Connell Street, at the foot of North Earl Street, stands a life-sized statue of James Joyce, who happily poses for photos with admiring tourists. (Joyce would also find a bust of himself in St. Stephen's Green, a Liffey bridge named after him, but the thing that would probably tickle his degenerate heart the most is "James Joyce Street"—the erstwhile Corporation Street—right smack in the middle of "Nighttown," Dublin's ancient Red Light District.) Apparently he has come a long way in the eyes of the state since he declared on leaving Ireland: "Silence, exile, cunning."

James Joyce and Samuel Beckett share many things: both were Dubliners, groundbreaking literary innovators, and exiles to Paris, where Beckett served for a while as Joyce's amanuensis when he was working on Finnegans Wake.

James Joyce:

"A man of genius makes no mistakes; his errors are volitional and are the portals of discovery."

"Writing in English is the most ingenious torture ever devised for sins committed in previous lives. The English reading public explains the reason why."

Samuel Beckett:

"James Joyce was a synthesizer, trying to bring in as much as he could. I am an analyzer, trying to leave out as much as I can."

"I write about myself with the same pencil and in the same exercise book as about him. It is no longer I, but another whose life is just beginning."

"Alas, no Irish [whiskey] here—only Vat 69, or still lousier Donats."
—SAMUEL BECKETT ON WHY HE COULD NOT PROPERLY CELEBRATE WINNING THE NOBEL PRIZE IN LITERATURE IN 1969

William Butler Yeats was the first Irishman to win the Nobel Prize in Literature in 1923:

"I consider that this honour has come to me less as an individual than as a representative of Irish literature, it is part of Europe's welcome to the Free State."

"The theatres of Dublin were empty buildings hired by the English travelling companies, and we wanted Irish plays and Irish players. When we thought of these plays we thought of everything that was romantic and poetical, because the nationalism we had called up—the nationalism every generation had called up in moments of discouragement—was romantic and poetical."

Seamus Heaney, following in the path set by Yeats, is the fourth Irishman to win the Nobel Prize in Literature:

"It's like being a little foothill at the bottom of a mountain range. You hope you just live up to it. It's extraordinary."—On winning the Nobel and residing in the company of Yeats, Shaw and Beckett.

"Write whatever you like!"

"I credit poetry for making this space-walk possible."

"In fact, in lyric poetry, truthfulness becomes recognizable as a ring of truth within the medium itself."

"The completely solitary self: that's where poetry comes from, and it gets isolated by crisis, and those crises are often very intimate also."

"I've always associated the moment of writing with a moment of lift, of joy, of unexpected reward."

"I always believed that whatever had to be written would somehow get itself written."

Paul Muldoon, Pulitzer Prize-winning poet from Northern Ireland:

"Words want to find chimes with each other; things want to connect."

"That's one of the great things about poetry; one realizes that one does one's little turn—that you're just part of the great crop, as it were."

"The point of poetry is to be acutely discomforting, to prod and provoke, to poke us in the eye, to punch us in the nose, to knock us off our feet, to take our breath away."

"If the poem has no obvious destination, there's a chance that we'll be all setting off on an interesting ride."

"Form is a straitjacket in the way that a straitjacket was a straitjacket for Houdini."

Nuala Ní Dhomhnaill, Gaelic poet:

"Irish is a language of beauty, historical significance, ancient roots, and an immense propensity for poetic expression through its everyday use."

"One of the things that causes me to get up in the morning is the desire to take Irish back from that grey-faced Irish revivalist male preserve."

• • •

"I dabbled in verse and it became my life."
—PATRICK KAVANAGH

• • •

"Wounds that hurt a poet's soul can rob him of renown"
—AOGÁN Ó RATHAILLE (1675–1729),
FROM "VALENTINE BROWN"

Colm Tóibín, writer:

"A novelist could probably run a military campaign with some success. They could certainly run a country."

"If a storyteller came up to me, I'd run away."

"I was brought up in a house where there was a great deal of silence."

"I wanted to be a poet as a child and I have a wall in my study dedicated to poetry books, all in alphabetical order, that reminds me daily of my failure."

"I have a rule that I don't drink in New York because I don't want to wake up with a hangover and not be able to work."

"Ending a novel is almost like putting a child to sleep —it can't be done abruptly."

"It's impossible for a creative artist to be either a Puritan or a Fascist, because both are a negation of the creative urge. The only things a creative artist can be opposed to are ugliness and injustice."
—Liam O'Flaherty

• • •

"The two hardest things about writing are starting and not stopping."
—Stewart O'Nan, novelist

• • •

"I would insist that poetry is a normal human activity and its proper concern all the things that happen to people."
—MICHAEL LONGLEY

There was no bigger celebrity/writer in the late 1950s and early '60s than Brendan Behan. His early works such as Borstal Boy *and the plays* The Hostage *and* The Quare Fellow *were works of genius. But drink took its hold and he was left to dictating his final "books" into a tape recorder because he could no longer write. He died in Dublin in 1964 at the age of 41.*

"Critics are like eunuchs in a harem; they know how it's done, they've seen it done every day, but they're unable to do it themselves."

"I am a drinker with writing problems."

"Shakespeare said pretty well everything and what he left out, James Joyce, with a judge from meself, put in."

"An author's first duty is to let down his country."

"We learn from failure, not from success!"
—BRAM STOKER, *DRACULA*

• • •

"Mad Ireland hurt you into poetry."
—W.H. AUDEN, "IN MEMORY OF W.B. YEATS"

• • •

"But with writers, there's nothing wrong with melancholy. It's an important color in writing."
—PAUL MCCARTNEY

*John F. Kennedy knew something about books.
He won the Pulitzer Prize in 1957 for* Profiles in Courage:

"If more politicians knew poetry, and more poets knew politics, I am convinced the world would be a little better place in which to live."

"Let us welcome controversial books and controversial authors."

"Censorship of anything, at any time, in any place, on whatever pretense, has always been and always will be the last report of the boob and the bigot."
—EUGENE O'NEILL

• • •

"Just as it is true that a stream cannot rise above its source, so it is true that a national literature cannot rise above the moral level of the social conditions of the people from whom it derives its inspiration."
—JAMES CONNOLLY

Born on Westland Row in Dublin Oscar Wilde went on to achieve wide literary fame—and other forms of infamy—in the late 19th century. His wit and sagacity has not been dimmed in the century since his death.

"I hate vulgar realism in literature. The man who could call a spade a spade should be compelled to use one. It is the only thing he is fit for."

"I regard the theatre as the greatest of all art forms, the most immediate way in which a human being can share with another the sense of what it is to be a human being."

"All bad poetry springs from genuine feeling."

"A poet can survive everything but a misprint."

"If one cannot enjoy reading a book over and over again, there is no use in reading it at all."

"The books that the world calls immoral are books that show the world its own shame."

"There is no such thing as a moral or an immoral book. Books are well written, or badly written."

"Sodom and begorra."
—A Dublin wag on the difference between the Gate and Abbey Theatres

Edna O'Brien was born in County Clare in 1930. Like Joyce she had to flee Ireland after the publication of The Country Girls, *a controversial look at Irish sexual and social mores after World War II.*

"Writing is like carrying a fetus."

"My hand does the work and I don't have to think; in fact, were I to think, it would stop the flow. It's like a dam in the brain that bursts."

"Writers really live in the mind and in hotels of the soul."

Apparently, great writing minds think alike:

"Everywhere I go I'm asked if I think the university stifles writers. My opinion is that they don't stifle enough of them."
—KATE O'BRIEN

• • •

"Everywhere I go, I'm asked if I think the universities stifle writers. My opinion is that they don't stifle enough of them. There's many a bestseller that could have been prevented by a good teacher."
—FLANNERY O'CONNOR

Flannery O'Connor's Catholicism played an important part in her writings of the American South. Lupus took her life at the age of 39.

"I am not afraid that the book will be controversial; I'm afraid it will not be controversial."

"When a book leaves your hands, it belongs to God. He may use it to save a few souls or to try a few others, but I think that for the writer to worry is to take over God's business."

"The writer should never be ashamed of staring. There is nothing that does not require his attention."

"The basis of art is truth, both in matter and in mode."

"Writing a novel is a terrible experience, during which the hair often falls out and the teeth decay."

"The writer operates at a peculiar crossroads where time and place and eternity somehow meet. His problem is to find that location."

"The writer can choose what he writes about but he cannot choose what he is able to make live."

"Writing is turning life's worst moments into money."
—J. P. DONLEAVY

Jimmy Breslin:

"Media, the plural of mediocrity."

"Rage is the only quality which has kept me, or anybody I have ever studied, writing columns for newspapers."

"There is only one admirable form of the imagination: the imagination that is so intense that it creates a new reality, that it makes things happen."
—SEAN O'FAOLAIN

John O'Hara:

"An artist is his own fault."

"Little old ladies of both sexes. Why do I let them bother me?"

"I write because I like to make things and the only things
I am good at making things with are words."
—P. J. O'ROURKE

Peter O'Toole:

"If I'm not at my study by 10:00, 10:30, forget it.
I can't write a word."

"Writing is a kind of performing art, and I can't sit down to write
unless I'm dressed. I don't mean dressed in a suit, but dressed
well and comfortably and I have to be shaved and bathed."

*Frank McCourt burst on the literary scene at the age of
66 with the publication of* Angela's Ashes, *which won the
Pulitzer Prize in 1997.*

"I think I settled on the title [*Angela's Ashes*] before
I ever wrote the book."

"I've been writing in notebooks for 40 years or so."

"I just have to proceed as usual. No matter what happens, nothing helps with the writing of the next book."

"Books! I dunno if I ever told you this, but books are the greatest gift one person can give another."
—BONO

Anne McCaffrey, Sci-fi/Fantasy author:

"But I will say that living in Ireland has changed the cadence and fullness of speech, since the Irish love words and use as many of them in a sentence as possible."

"A good story is a good story no matter who wrote it."

F. Scott Fitzgerald, like Mary McCarthy, grew up in Catholic Minnesota. He was a card-carrying member of the "Lost Generation" who called Paris their home in the 1920s. He once wrote "Show me a hero and I'll write you a tragedy" —he could have been writing about himself. He died of the drink at the age of 44.

"You can stroke people with words."

"Cut out all these exclamation points. An exclamation point is like laughing at your own joke."

"All good writing is swimming under water and holding your breath."

"You don't write because you want to say something, you write because you have something to say."

"An author ought to write for the youth of his own generation, the critics of the next, and the schoolmaster of ever afterwards."

"To write it, it took three months; to conceive it three minutes; to collect the data in it all my life."

James Plunkett's most famous work is Strumpet City, *about the hostile Dublin of James Larkin, torn by labor unrest, just prior to the Great War and the Easter Rising of 1916. He once said he wrote "from memories, persistent memories, which I want to write in order to exorcise them."*

"[Writing is] the most crucifying work. When I'm at it I keep asking why in the name of Christ am I doing this to myself when I could be taking my ease?"

"But I know bloody well that if I put a novel aside without finishing it, I will be utterly bloody miserable."

"Why does a writer write? My own view is that it is his attempt to understand his own memoires. Memory, I firmly believe, is the source of all insight, and literature is conceived out of the constant contemplation of those images which accumulate in the memory and persist in making their presence felt throughout the whole of the writer's life."

"[I]t is a truth of literature that nothing much happens to a writer after the age of twenty or so that will affect his work; the small store of material which informs the imagination for the rest of his life is made up of the remembered experiences of childhood and youth."

Hugh Leonard is one of Ireland's most prolific writers and is remembered especially for Da, *his play about his father, which opened at the Olympia Theatre during the Dublin Theatre Festival in 1973. It starred the fine American comedic actor, John McGiver.*

"My father I liked, but it was only after his death that I got to know him by writing the play [*Da*]."

"Gossip is more popular than literature."

"I think with every writer there are two people there."

"I'm a writer, and what I do is write. I wasn't able to do anything else."

"It's a natural thing for people to say, you know, Who's in this book? I find myself getting a little defensive. People come along and I'm waiting for that first question."

John Millington Synge:

"I'm a good scholar when it comes to reading but a blotting kind of writer when you give me a pen."

"In a good play every speech should be as fully flavored as a nut or apple."

The prolific, opinionated—and at times prickly—Roddy Doyle has brought the world such novels (and films) as The Commitments, The Snapper, *and* The Van.

"*Ulysses* could have done with a good editor. You know people are always putting *Ulysses* in the top ten books ever written but I doubt that any of those people were really moved by it."

"Fuck was the best word. The most dangerous word. You couldn't whisper it. Fuck was always too loud, too late to stop it, it burst in the air above you and fell slowly right over your head. There was total silence, nothing but Fuck floating down."
—FROM *PADDY CLARKE HA HA HA*

"I tend to plan as I write. And I want to leave myself open and the character open to keep on going until it seems to be the time to stop."

"I see people in terms of dialogue and I believe that people are their talk."

"Could a man live by it, it were not unpleasant employment to be a poet."
—OLIVER GOLDSMITH

Thomas Moore:

"Though an angel should write, still 'tis devils must print."

"True change takes place in the imagination."

"Originality does not consist in saying what no one has ever said before, but in saying exactly what you think yourself."
—JAMES STEPHENS

• • •

"Writing is learning to say nothing, more cleverly each day."
—WILLIAM ALLINGHAM, POET

• • •

"Find enough clever things to say, and you're a Prime Minister; write them down and you're a Shakespeare."
—GEORGE BERNARD SHAW

Edmund Burke:

"Poetry is the art of substantiating shadows, and of lending existence to nothing."

"To read without reflecting is like eating without digesting."

"Write how you want, the critic shall show the
world you could have written better."
—OLIVER GOLDSMITH

*Margaret Mitchell was another American Southern writer who had
a frank outlook on life—especially about sex. She only wrote one
book, but what a book. It was called* Gone with the Wind.

"In a weak moment, I have written a book."

"I do not write with ease, nor am I ever pleased with anything
I write. And so I rewrite."

"Why will people persist in reading strange meanings into the
simplest of story? Is it not enough that a writer can entertain
for a few hours with narrative without being suspected of
'significances' or symbolism or 'social trends'?"

*Like Frank McCourt, Mary McCarthy survived a horrid Catholic
childhood and went on to write about it. Her feud with Lillian
Hellman ("Every word she writes is a lie, including 'and' and 'the'.")
made for delicious tabloid headlines at the end of both of their lives.*

"I am putting real plums into an imaginary cake."

"A novelist is an elephant, but an elephant who
must pretend to forget."

"The suspense of a novel is not only in the reader, but in the
novelist, who is intensely curious about what will happen
to the hero."

"The theater is the only branch of art much cared for by people of wealth; like canasta, it does away with the bother of talk after dinner."

"We all live in suspense from day to day; in other words, you are the hero of your own story."

14

♘

Monie$ & W€a£th

"There is only one class in the community that thinks
more about money than the rich, and that is the poor.
The poor can think of nothing else."
—OSCAR WILDE

• • •

To say the Irish are ambivalent about money and wealth is an
understatement. Long on poverty and joblessness, Ireland has driven
her native sons out of the country, penniless, as a matter of habit.
And the Catholic Church has reinforced how admirable poverty is by
always promoting the notion that "rewards" will be in the "next life."
That's all well and good, but a bit of grub and a pint of grog demand
money in this vale of tears. The Bible may proclaim "For the love of
money is the root of all kinds of evil," (1 Timothy 6:10) but the Irish
have always had an eye on the wallet wherever they have roamed.

*Poverty demands that. Their most famous revolutionary, Michael
Collins, was also their first Minister for Finance. Michael Collins
could count—much to the chagrin of the British—and he protected
the wealth of the nation at the point of a gun. And like Collins, the
Irish have shown they too know how to count, but they are wise
enough to know that all that shines is not gold. They may lustily gleam
at the dollar-pound-and-euro signs—but since the recent looting of
the nation's fortune by the rancid bankers and real estate developers—
that gleam is filled with cynicism. They found that their vaunted
"Celtic Tiger" was actually a castrated pussycat. Fixed, but good.*

"Let me tell you about the very rich. They are different from you and me. They possess and enjoy early, and it does something to them, makes them soft, where we are hard, cynical where we are trustful, in a way that, unless you were born rich, it is very difficult to understand."
—F. Scott Fitzgerald, from his short story "The Rich Boy" (1926)

Sean O'Casey:

"Money does not make you happy but it quiets the nerves."

"Wealth often takes away chances from men as well as poverty. There is none to tell the rich to go on striving, for a rich man makes the law that hallows and hollows his own life."

"If a free society cannot help the many who are poor, it cannot save the few who are rich."
—John F. Kennedy

• • •

"There are 200 million poor in the world who would gladly take the vow of poverty if they could eat, dress and have a home like I do."
—Bishop Fulton J. Sheen

Oscar Wilde was born into wealth, wanted for nothing at the apogee of his career, yet died in poverty in Paris at the age of 46:

"When I was young I thought that money was the most important thing in life; now that I am old I know that it is."

"No man is rich enough to buy back his past."

"It is better to have a permanent income than to be fascinating."

"It is only by not paying one's bills that one can hope to live in the memory of the commercial classes."

"I am dying beyond my means."

The story (as told by Sam Beckett) may be apocryphal, but when W.B. Yeats was told he had won the Nobel Prize in Literature in 1923 by a very solemn Lord Mayor of Dublin he was said to have spit out, "Yes, yes, just tell me what it's worth! How much will I get?"

• • •

"It seems that the fiction writer has a revolting attachment to the poor, for even when he writes about the rich, he is more concerned with what they lack than with what they have."
—FLANNERY O'CONNOR

• • •

Why do you rob banks? "Because that's where the money is."
—WILLIE SUTTON

• • •

"Ninety percent I'll spend on good times, women, and Irish whiskey. The other ten percent I'll probably waste."
—TUG MCGRAW, RELIEF PITCHER, NEW YORK METS

• • •

"I spent a lot of money on booze, birds, and fast cars. The rest I just squandered."
—GEORGE BEST

• • •

"God shows his contempt for wealth by the kind of person he selects to receive it."
—AUSTIN O'MALLEY

• • •

"It is better to spend money like there's no tomorrow than to
spend tonight like there's no money."
—P.J. O'Rourke

Errol Flynn:

"Any man who has $10,000 left when he
dies is a failure."

"My problem lies in reconciling my gross habits
with my net income."

Oliver Goldsmith:

"Law grinds the poor, and rich men rule the law."

"The jests of the rich are ever successful."

"Where wealth accumulates, men decay."

Edmund Burke:

"Frugality is founded on the principle that all riches have limits."

"It is the interest of the commercial world that wealth should be found everywhere."

"If we command our wealth, we shall be rich and free; if our wealth commands us, we are poor indeed."

"Mere parsimony is not economy. Expense, and great expense, may be an essential part in true economy."

"Clothes make the poor invisible. America has the best-dressed poverty the world has ever known."
—MICHAEL HARRINGTON

• • •

"Starting out to make money is the greatest mistake in life. Do what you feel you have a flair for doing, and if you are good enough at it, the money will come."
—GREER GARSON, ACTRESS

15

Politics: Vote Early, Vote Often

"Our Irish ancestors believed in magic, prayers, trickery, browbeating, and bullying. I think it would be fair to sum that list up as 'Irish politics.'"
—FLANN O'BRIEN

• • •

If there's one profession—this side of the priesthood—that's attached to the Irish, it is the art of politics. It comes natural to them. They get to stand up in front of people and talk. They get to jeer their opponents. They get to look serious as the national anthem is being played—all the time thinking of how to shake down high-hat donors at $10,000-a-drink cocktail parties. The Irish in America learned early that those in power ruled the roost. They discovered the power of being policemen and firemen and aldermen. They learned it is better to give orders than to receive

*them. And they learned, in conjunction with the Catholic Church,
how important it was to support their people—and the next
generation of immigrants who were to follow—by controlling the
ballot box. As the years progressed they have fanned out to embrace
every political attitude—liberal, conservative, socialist, and fascist.
Some have been magnetic, some have been fatuous.
Few have been boring.*

"All politics is local."
—THOMAS P. (TIP) O'NEILL, FORMER SPEAKER
OF THE HOUSE (D-MA)

*Eugene McCarthy was the former Democratic United States
Senator from Minnesota. He was most famous for his presidential
run in 1968 against Lyndon Johnson and the Vietnam War. He was
a former seminarian and a published poet. His slant on politics
belied a cynical Celtic outlook:*

"Being in politics is like being a football coach. You have to be
smart enough to understand the game, and dumb enough to
think it's important."

"It is dangerous for a national candidate to say things
that people might remember."

"No man could be equipped for the presidency if he has never
been tempted by one of the seven cardinal sins."

When Michigan Governor George Romney, running for president in 1968, declared he had been "brainwashed" about the Vietnam War, Gene McCarthy responded that in Romney's case, "A light rinse would have been sufficient."

George Washington Plunkitt, Tammany Hall politician, was a man who knew the difference between "honest graft" and "dishonest graft":

"There's an honest graft, and I'm an example of how it works. I might sum up the whole thing by sayin': 'I seen my opportunities and I took' em.'"

"I am the law!"
—Frank Hague, mayor of Jersey City, New Jersey

Before Eugene McCarthy there was another Senator McCarthy, Joseph, a Republican from Wisconsin. Few politicians leave their name as a stain on the political landscape, but "Tailgunner Joe," as he liked to refer to himself in his campaign literature, hit the jackpot:

"The State Department is infested with communists. I have here in my hand a list of 205—a list of names that were made known to the Secretary of State as being members of the Communist Party and who nevertheless are still working and shaping policy in the State Department."

"McCarthyism is Americanism with its sleeves rolled."

Before there was John F. Kennedy there was Alfred E. Smith, the Irish-Catholic governor of New York. In 1928 he ran on the Democratic ticket for President of the United States. The prejudice leveled at him was nauseating. Reporter Frederick William observed that Smith was defeated by "The Three P's: Prohibition, Prejudice, and Prosperity." Many believed that if Al Smith was elected, the Pope would be moving into the White House. Al was not the smoothest politician, but he paved the way for JFK.

"The Brooklyn Bridge and I grew up together."

"I summarize my creed as an American Catholic. I believe in the worship of God according to the faith and practice of the Roman Catholic Church. I recognize no power in the institutions of my church to interfere with the operation of the Constitution of the United States or the enforcement of the law of the land. I believe in absolute freedom of conscience for all men and in equality of all churches, all sects, and all beliefs before the law as a matter of right and not as a matter of favor. I believe in the absolute separation of church and state and in the strict enforcement of the provisions of the Constitution of the United States."

"When the going gets tough, the tough get going."
—JOSEPH P. KENNEDY, FATHER OF JFK

• • •

"Joe Kennedy was a reactionary… Every Jew in Boston knew that old Joe Kennedy was an anti-Semite."
—TIP O'NEILL, *MAN OF THE HOUSE*

• • •

"It's not the Pope I'm worried about—it's the Pop!"
—HARRY TRUMAN ON WHY HE DIDN'T INITIALLY SUPPORT
JOHN F. KENNEDY FOR PRESIDENT IN 1960

• • •

"I've had a tough time learning how to act like a congressman.
Today I accidentally spent some of my own money."
—JOSEPH P. KENNEDY III, GRANDSON OF JOE KENNEDY

• • •

"Growing up in politics I know that women decide all elections because we do all the work."
—CAROLINE KENNEDY, ALSO JOE KENNEDY'S GRANDCHILD

• • •

"There was a moment of silence, as neither of us wanted to hang up. Then I said, 'Jerry, isn't this a wonderful country? Here we can talk like this and we can be friends, and eighteen months from now I'll be going around the country kicking your ass in.'"
—TIP O'NEILL WHEN HIS FRIEND, GERALD FORD,
BECAME PRESIDENT OF THE UNITED STATES

Oliver St. John Gogarty was the friend of James Joyce (he's the avatar for "Stately Plump Buck Mulligan" in Ulysses*), the physician to W.B. Yeats, friend of Michael Collins, Irish Senator, poet, writer, and wit:*

"Politics is the chloroform of the Irish people,
or rather the hashish."
—FROM *AS I WAS GOING DOWN SACKVILLE STREET*

• • •

"Every time Eamon de Valera contradicts himself,
he's right!"

"Mothers all want their sons to grow up to be president, but they
don't want them to become politicians in the process."
—JOHN F. KENNEDY

• • •

"It has been said that politics is the second oldest profession.
I have learned that it bears a striking resemblance to the first."
—RONALD REAGAN

• • •

"Keep your enemies in front of you."
—CHRIS MATTHEWS

• • •

"Forgive your enemies, but never forget their names."
—JOHN F. KENNEDY

• • •

"The majority of the members of the Irish parliament are professional politicians, in the sense that otherwise they would not be given jobs minding mice at crossroads."
—FLANN O'BRIEN

• • •

"Chicago is the Irish capital of the mid-west. A city where it was once said you could stand on 79th street and hear the brogue of every county in Ireland. So naturally, a politician like me craved a slot in the St Patrick's Day parade. The problem was not many people knew me or could not even pronounce my name. I told them it was a Gaelic name—they didn't believe me."
—BARACK OBAMA

• • •

"Nothing is politically right which is morally wrong."
—DANIEL O'CONNELL

• • •

"Politics is a choice of enemas. You're gonna get it up the ass, no matter what you do."
—GEORGE V. HIGGINS, NOVELIST

• • •

"The walls are raised against honest men in civic life."
—William Cardinal O'Connell

• • •

"I am not a witch!"
—Christine O'Donnell, Republican candidate
for the U.S. Senate in Delaware

• • •

"A speech is poetry: cadence, rhythm, imagery, sweep!
A speech reminds us that words, like children, have the
power to make dance the dullest beanbag of a heart."
—Peggy Noonan

• • •

"The statesman shears the sheep; the politician skins them."
—Austin O'Malley

• • •

"Politics is not a bad profession. If you succeed there are many
rewards; if you disgrace yourself you can always write a book."
—Ronald Reagan

• • •

"You can't trust politicians. It doesn't matter who makes a
political speech. It's all lies—and it applies to any rock star who
wants to make a political speech as well."
—Bob Geldof

Joe Biden is the 47th Vice President of the United States. He is Irish on his mother's side with roots in Derry and Louth. His U.S. Secret Service codename is "Celtic." He is known for being outspoken, making gaffes, but he sometimes manages to cut through all the political bull and nail things right on:

"This is a big fucking deal!"
—BIDEN TO PRESIDENT OBAMA ON THE
PASSAGE OF OBAMACARE

"You want to know whether we're better off? I've got a little bumper sticker for you: Osama bin Laden is dead and General Motors is alive."

"There's only three things he mentions in a sentence—a noun, a verb, and 9/11."
—BIDEN'S QUOTE THAT BASICALLY ENDED RUDY GIULIANI'S
POLITICAL CAREER

O'Leary, O'Reilly, O'Hare, and O'Hara/There's no one as Irish as Barack O'Bama
—THE CORRIGAN BROTHERS SONG ABOUT
BARACK OBAMA

• • •

"My name is Barack Obama, of the Moneygall Obamas, and I've come home to find the apostrophe that we lost somewhere along the way… We feel very much at home. I feel even more at home after that pint I had. I feel even warmer… Now I knew I had some roots across the Atlantic, but until recently I could not unequivocally claim that I was one of those Irish-Americans. But now, if you believe the Corrigan brothers, there is no one more Irish than me."
—BARACK OBAMA, DUBLIN 2011

Edmund Burke returns:

"All government, indeed every human benefit and enjoyment, every virtue, and every prudent act, is founded on compromise and barter."

"Politics and the pulpit are terms that have little agreement."

"Magnanimity in politics is not seldom the truest wisdom; and a great empire and little minds go ill together."

"When the leaders choose to make themselves bidders at an auction of popularity, their talents, in the construction of the state, will be of no service. They will become flatterers instead of legislators; the instruments, not the guides, of the people."

"In politics, it seems, retreat is honorable if dictated
by military considerations and shameful if even
suggested for ethical reasons."
—MARY MCCARTHY

• • •

Three Mayors: A Rogue, an Icon, and a Boss

*As the Irish fled the Great Famine of the 1840s they landed in
American cities—heavily in Boston, New York, and Philadelphia.
They also traveled towards the plains, occupying Chicago, St. Louis,
Kansas City, and kept going until they got to Los Angeles and San
Francisco. At first these immigrants were thought of as little more
than drunken chimpanzees (see the art work of Thomas Nast), but
through the Catholic Church and ward politics they learned how
to overcome prejudice and begin governing. Politics was the key as
they took control of the cities they had invaded, sometimes less than
a half-century before. As Democratic political machines were built
up, three 20th century mayors stuck out for different reasons.*

The Rogue

*In New York in the 1920s there was James J. Walker, aka
"Jimmy" and "Beau James." He was known as the "Mayor of the
Jazz Age." Some say he was a crook, but history records him
as a lovable rogue:*

"I never knew a girl who was ruined by a book."

"A reformer is a guy who rides through the sewer in a glass bottom boat."

"There are three things a man must do alone. Be born, die, and testify."

"I'd rather be a lamppost in New York than mayor of Chicago."

The Icon

To the north, in Boston, home of the Brahmin, they had a mayor named James Michael Curley. "When the good Lord made James Michael Curley," said Tip O'Neill, "He broke the mold." In Edwin O'Connor's great novel of Americana, The Last Hurrah, *Curley served as the avatar for Frank Skeffington:*

"Every time you do a favor for a constituent, you make nine enemies and one ingrate."

"The day of the Puritan has passed; the Anglo-Saxon is a joke; a new and better America is here."

"…[A]s spectacular as a four-day-old codfish and as colorful as a lump of mud." Curley on one of his political opponents

The Boss

Out in Chicago, for two decades starting in the 1950s, Richard
J. Daley ruled the roost. Pulitzer Prize-winning columnist Mike
Royko called him "Boss"—and he wasn't confusing him with Bruce
Springsteen. Nothing moved in the Windy City without Daley's say-
so. Daley was a rock-hard Democrat, and by 1960 John F. Kennedy
was his candidate for president. Come election night Daley was
sitting on the vote in Cook County, waiting to see how many votes
downstate the Republicans were going to steal. Jack Kennedy, in
Hyannisport, was getting nervous because he desperately needed
Illinois' electoral votes to win the presidency. He called Daley up
and asked him what was going on. "With a little bit of luck and
the help of a few close friends," assured Daley, "you're going to
carry Illinois." One always had the impression that those "few close
friends" were voting from local cemeteries. I have no problems with
that. The Irish fought long and hard to win the right to vote—even
after death! His bulldog of an Irish face became a symbol of the
divisiveness that engulfed America in the 1960s. The mayor, a
master of the malaprop, had a way of making things worse than
they actually were:

"The policeman isn't there to create disorder; the policeman is
there to preserve disorder."

"We are proud to have with us the poet *lariat* of Chicago."

"They have vilified me, they have crucified me; yes, they have
even criticized me."

"What is inherently wrong with the word 'politician' if the fellow has devoted his life to holding public office and trying to do something for his people?"

"Good government is good politics."

"Even the Lord had skeptical members of His party."

"Look at our Lord's disciples. One denied Him; one doubted Him; one betrayed Him. If our Lord couldn't have perfection, how are you going to have it in city government?"

"A newspaper is the lowest thing there is."

16

U

Two 20th Century
Irish-American Presidents

*"Our spirit is eternally refreshed by Irish story and Irish song;
our public life by the humor and heart and dedication of
servants with names like Kennedy and Reagan."*
—BARACK OBAMA

• • •

*One was the scion of a wealthy Boston businessman, the other
a product of the Hollywood star system. One a Catholic,
the other a Protestant. One a liberal Democrat,
the other a conservative Republican.*

*Yet, John F. Kennedy and Ronald Reagan had many things in
common. Both were tremendous communicators. Reagan, in fact,
was known as the "Great Communicator."*

Two 20th Century Irish-American Presidents

Reagan was blessed with that certain knack that allowed him to always nail that sound bite:

"Mr. Gorbachev, tear down this wall!"

Kennedy wasn't too shabby himself. He could handle a sound bite before anyone knew what a sound bite was:

"Ask not what your country can do for you, ask what you can do for your country."

Both were also virulent anti-Communists, with Kennedy facing down Khrushchev over Cuba and Reagan getting great credit for the eventual collapse of the Soviet Union.

Kennedy also held the high moral ground in the fight for civil rights in America, and much of the civil rights legislation passed after his death by President Lyndon Johnson was written during the Kennedy Administration.

Both knew how to make deals: Kennedy with Khrushchev; Reagan with fellow Irishman—the very liberal Speaker of the House—Tip O'Neill. Kennedy's deal resulted in the Nuclear Test Ban Treaty of 1963. Reagan's helped buck up the Social Security system in the 1980s.

Both were political philosophers who knew how to enjoy a good laugh. Both were sons of Ireland, very aware of their Irish backgrounds. And both returned to Ireland as president.

John F. Kennedy:

Kennedy returned to Ireland a national hero. A Catholic who became President of the United States! "He's one of us!" was the local consensus. But during his visit in June 1963 he remembered his family's humble beginning as he addressed the crowds in County Wexford, showing a self-deprecating wit that left the crowd howling: "If [my grandfather] hadn't left, I'd be working over here at the Albatross [fertilizer] Company." As he left Ireland for the last time he said of his next visit "I'll come back in the springtime," but he had already lived his last spring.

But the thing that still stands out about Kennedy fifty years after his death was his quick, whimsical sense of humor. In fact, Kennedy himself probably gave the best definition about the importance of laughter ever: "There are three things which are real: God, human folly, and laughter. The first two are beyond our comprehension. So we must do what we can with the third." Politicians today practice their spontaneous witty responses, their "zingers." Kennedy didn't have to do that; his were spontaneous, right off the top of his head:

When asked by a little boy how he became a war hero, Kennedy replied: "It was absolutely involuntary. They sank my boat."

"I hope you keep them."—To Soviet Premier Nikita Khrushchev after Khrushchev showed him his Lenin Peace Medals

Asked why the Republicans pulled its "Truth Squad" during the 1960 presidential campaign: "He told the truth."

"I have just received the following wire from my generous daddy: 'Dear Jack—Don't buy a single vote more than is necessary—I'll be damned if I'm going to pay for a landslide.'"

"Whether I serve one or two terms in the Presidency, I will find myself at the end of that period at what might be called the awkward age—too old to begin a new career and too young to write my memoirs."

"I have a nice home, the office is close by, and the pay is good." —On being President

"I don't see anything wrong with giving him a little legal experience before he goes out to practice law."—On the appointment of his brother Robert as U.S. Attorney General

Kennedy was once asked what his favorite song was: "Hail to the Chief," he impishly replied. He had a special affection for "The Boys of Wexford," a rebel song about the Rising of 1798:

> We are the boys of Wexford,
> Who fought with heart and hand
> To burst in twain the galling chain
> And free our native land.

After his death, it was to be the theme song for the *Profiles in Courage* television program, based on his Pulitzer Prize-winning book.

Senator Kennedy's performance at the 1960 Al Smith Dinner in New York City just prior to the election still elicits laughter:

"Cardinal Spellman is the only man so widely respected in American politics that he could bring together amicably, at the same banquet table, for the first time in this campaign, two political leaders who are increasingly apprehensive about the November election who have long eyed each other suspiciously, and who have disagreed so strongly, both publicly and privately— Vice President Nixon and Governor Rockefeller."

• • •

"Mr. Nixon, like the rest of us, has had his troubles in this campaign. At one point even the *Wall Street Journal* was criticizing his tactics. That is like the *Observatore Romano* criticizing the Pope."

"On this matter of experience, I had announced earlier this year that if successful I would not consider campaign contributions as a substitute for experience in appointing ambassadors. Ever since I made that statement I have not received one single cent from my father."

Ronald Reagan:

As noted before, no one could beat Reagan for the succinct, yet powerful sound bite. And you challenged him at your own risk:

"Well, there you go again."

"Recession is when a neighbor loses his job. Depression is when you lose yours."

"Trust, but verify."

"How can a president not be an actor?"

"Trees cause more pollution than automobiles."

"I've noticed that everyone who is for
abortion has already been born."

"I have only one thing to say to the tax increasers:
Go ahead, make my day."

*In his first inauguration address Reagan famously declared that
"government is not the solution to our problem." It was a theme
that he would frequently return to:*

"No government ever voluntarily reduces itself in size.
Government programs, once launched, never disappear. Actually,
a government bureau is the nearest thing to eternal life we'll ever
see on this earth!"

"Government is like a baby. An alimentary canal
with a big appetite at one end and no sense of
responsibility at the other."

"The taxpayer—that's someone who works for the federal
government but doesn't have to take the civil service
examination."

"The most terrifying words in the English language are:
'I'm from the government and I'm here to help.'"

"One way to make sure crime doesn't pay would be
to let the government run it."

"I have wondered at times what the Ten Commandments would have looked like if Moses had run them through the U.S. Congress."

With the perfect timing of the experienced actor he was, Reagan went about turning a negative—his age—into a positive. Walter Mondale is still feeling Reagan's bite:

"I want you to know that also I will not make age an issue of this campaign. I am not going to exploit, for political purposes, my opponent's youth and inexperience."—During a 1984 presidential debate with Democratic presidential nominee Walter Mondale

"Thomas Jefferson once said, 'We should never judge a president by his age, only by his works.' And ever since he told me that, I stopped worrying."

"I never drink coffee at lunch. I find it keeps me awake for the afternoon."

"It's true hard work never killed anybody, but I figure, why take the chance?"

"No matter what time it is, wake me, even if it's in the middle of a Cabinet meeting."

Like Kennedy, Reagan was the target of an assassin in 1981, but, unlike Kennedy, he was lucky enough to survive.

"I hope you're all Republicans."—Speaking to surgeons as he entered the operating room

"Honey, I forgot to duck."—To his wife, Nancy

17

Drink

God invented whiskey to keep the Irish from ruling the world.
—Irish Saying

• • •

The Irish and drink—the ultimate love-hate relationship.

*Their love of the drink has been parodied, sung about, used to
shame, but also used to uplift a forlorn people. Drink has played a
central place in Irish life. The public house—the Pub—is important
to the Irish because they celebrate there, they plot revolution there,
they think there, and they also drown their sorrows there. These
are the sorrows of a country long on occupation, short on jobs, and
haunted by famine, immigration, and revolution. Drink has always
been the obvious—and easy—solution.*

The Irish invented whiskey (no one knows how they missed out on the potato booze, vodka). They called it uisce beatha—*the "water of life." The English could not understand what the Irish were talking about in their language, so* uisce beatha—*pronounced "ishkey-baha"—was corrupted into English as "whiskey." That was a start, then Arthur Guinness came around, mistakenly burnt some of his beer, and Guinness Stout was born on the banks of the River Liffey, as the label on the bottle says, in 1759.*

According to the World Health Organization, Ireland ranks at #15 on their list of countries measured by alcoholic consumption.

Drink

This may not sound that impressive except when it is compared to the nation that invented that grand social study known as Prohibition. The United States is ranked at #57 by WHO. Of course there is the difference in population size. Ireland's population is under seven million while the U.S. has soared well past 300 million. There seems to be a Hertz-Avis battle-in-reverse of the livers going on here.

Alcoholism in Ireland in the mid-19th century was such a problem that Father Theobald Matthew came along and invented "The Pledge," an oath that promised that Irish lips would remain virgin to demon alcohol. Father Matthew also had an audience in America where he was embraced by Protestants, perhaps because they were terrified by all the drunken Irish suddenly in their midst.

Obviously, alcoholism has been hard on the Irish. Revolution has been betrayed by it. Families have been destroyed by it. Writers like F. Scott Fitzgerald and Brendan Behan have been cut down in mid-life and had their talent eviscerated by it. So it is with a wary eye that the Irish view booze. When someone goes into rehab they call it going to "whiskey school." The sad fact is that some can handle it and some can't. And there's only one way to find out.

And alcohol also has an important place in the mind of the deeply Catholic Ireland. The priest during the mass changes wine—not sparkling water—into the blood of Jesus Christ. James Joyce's last book is about the redemptive power of alcohol. Finnegans Wake *is the tale of Tim Finnegan who dies and at his wake is revived when a barrel of whiskey explodes on him. The "water of life."*

Resurrection, Irish style.

F. Scott Fitzgerald fought a long and losing fight with alcohol.
He was dead at 44:

"First you take a drink, then the drink takes a drink, then the drink takes you."

"I've been drunk for about a week now, and I thought it might sober me up to sit in a library."

"Often people display a curious respect for a man drunk, rather like the respect of simple races for the insane… There is something awe-inspiring in one who has lost all inhibitions."

"An Irish homosexual is one who prefers women to drink."
—SEAN O'FAOLAIN

• • •

"Give an Irishman lager for a month, and he's a dead man. An Irishman is lined with copper, and the beer corrodes it. But whiskey polishes the copper and is the saving of him."
—MARK TWAIN

• • •

"When I die I want to decompose in a barrel of porter and have it served in all the pubs in Dublin."
—J. P. DONLEAVY

• • •

Drink

"And I said to myself, *I'm never going to do this again.*
I finished my drink. It was the last one I ever had."

—Pete Hamill, from *A Drinking Life*

• • •

"One drink is too many for me and a thousand not enough."
—Brendan Behan

• • •

"He had a habit of remarking to bartenders that he didn't see any sense in mixing whiskey with water since the whiskey was already wet."
—Joseph Mitchell

• • •

"I drink because I'm thirsty."
—Shane MacGowan, musician

• • •

"I was the worst barman who ever lived. My pints of Guinness were unholy."
—Colm Tóibín, writer

James Larkin:

"I never stood in a public house bar and alcoholic drink never touched my lips."

"I have raised the morals and sobriety of the people."

George Best, Belfast footballer:

"I've stopped drinking, but only while I'm asleep."

Drink

"I was in for 10 hours and had 40 pints—beating my previous record by 20 minutes." —*On his blood transfusions during his liver transplant*

Ronnie Drew of the Dubliners was on the wagon. He felt the need to have a drink and went into a pub. The only other patron in the bar turned to Ronnie and commented, "I thought you were off the drink." "I am," Ronnie replied, "but I have a gin and tonic every now and again. I find it helps me to mind my own business. Would you like one?"

"Alcohol is the anesthesia by which we endure the operation of life."
—GEORGE BERNARD SHAW

• • •

"One tequila, two tequila, three tequila, *floor*."
—GEORGE CARLIN

• • •

"I know I've got Irish blood because
I wake up every day with a hangover."
—NOEL GALLAGHER, MUSICIAN

• • •

"In a study, scientists report that drinking beer can be good for the liver. I'm sorry, did I say 'scientists?' I meant 'Irish people.'"
—TINA FEY

• • •

"Only Irish Coffee provides in a single glass all four essential food groups: alcohol, caffeine, sugar, and fat."
—ALEX LEVINE, MUSICIAN

• • •

"There two Irishmen were passing a pub—well, it could happen."
—FRANK CARSON, COMEDIAN

• • •

"C'mon, Moe. It's been St. Patrick's Day for hours now and I'm not drunk yet!"
—HOMER SIMPSON

• • •

"We are such things as rubbish is made of, so let's drink up and forget it."
—EUGENE O'NEILL, *LONG DAY'S JOURNEY INTO NIGHT*

• • •

"Work is the curse of the drinking classes."
—OSCAR WILDE

• • •

"I only use my sick days for hangovers and soap opera weddings."
—KATE O'BRIEN

• • •

"When you stop drinking, you have to deal with this marvelous personality that started you drinking in the first place."
—JIMMY BRESLIN

• • •

Drink

"I like my whiskey old and my women young."
—ERROL FLYNN

• • •

What butter and whiskey will not cure there's no cure for.
—IRISH PROVERB

• • •

"The problem with some people is that when
they aren't drunk they're sober."
—WILLIAM BUTLER YEATS

• • •

Drink is the curse of the land.
It makes you fight with your neighbor.
It makes you shoot at your landlord.
And it makes you *miss* him.
IRISH SAYING

• • •

"Let schoolmasters puzzle their brain with grammar, and
nonsense, and learning. Good liquor, I stoutly maintain, gives
genius a better discerning."
—OLIVER GOLDSMITH

• • •

"Hell, if I didn't drink or smoke, I'd win twenty games every year.
It's easy when you don't drink or smoke or horse around."
—WHITEY FORD, HALL OF FAME PITCHER

• • •

"Under the pressure of the cares and sorrows of our mortal condition, men have at all times, and in all countries, called in some physical aid to their moral consolations—wine, beer, opium, brandy, or tobacco."
—EDMUND BURKE

• • •

"I got quite bored, serving in the bar. Since I was there, the customers wouldn't talk about women, and with half their subject matter denied them, it was: horses, silence; horses, silence."
—BERNADETTE DEVLIN

18

♍

Death

Cast a cold eye/On life, on death/Horseman pass by
—W.B. YEATS

• • •

The Irish fascination with death probably goes hand-in-hand with their fascination of wakes. The Irish (Gaelic) word for wake is faire, *which is not surprising considering the Irish obsession with faeries and banshees. The purpose of the wake was to ascertain that the dead person was, in fact, dead, and did not awake. It was the job of the mourners to help the departed soul transition to their new life.*
I can remember my father, who grew up in very rural County Louth, telling ghost stories and long tales of digging graves for neighbors. My mother, a Dublin woman, swore by the "Three Knocks at the Door," which was a sign of imminent death. My father would tell her she was "full of pisterogs." My father was not

an Irish speaker, but Irish words would often color his vocabulary.
As an adult I learned that there was a basis in my father's
"pisterogs." It derives from the Irish word piseog, *which means*
"superstitious." So my father was right about his "pisterogs."
Now I often wonder if my mother was right about her
"Three Knocks."

• • •

Death

"Birth was the death of him."
—SAMUEL BECKETT

• • •

"No man is so old as to believe he cannot live one more year."
—SEAN O'CASEY

• • •

"There is no such thing as bad publicity—except your own obituary."
—BRENDAN BEHAN

• • •

"The rumors of my death have been greatly exaggerated."
—PAUL MCCARTNEY

• • •

Health and a long life to you.
Land without rent to you.
A child every year to you.
And if you can't go to heaven,
May you at least die in Ireland.
—IRISH TOAST

The one and only George Carlin:

"I was thinking about how people seem to read the Bible a whole lot more as they get older; then it dawned on me—they're cramming for their final exam."

"Death is caused by swallowing small amounts of saliva over a long period of time."

"At a formal dinner party, the person nearest death should always be seated closest to the bathroom."

"I'm always relieved when someone is delivering a eulogy and I realize I'm listening to it."

"Everybody loves you when you're six foot in the ground."
—JOHN LENNON

• • •

"I won't be buried at all, or cremated. I'm going to be stuffed and mounted."
—FRANK MCCOURT

• • •

"Biography lends to death a new terror."
—OSCAR WILDE

• • •

"I'm Irish. I think about death all the time."
—JACK NICHOLSON

• • •

Death

"Death is like a woman, in that it largely depends for
existence on the interest taken in it. We have to a
great extent invented Death."
—OLIVER ST. JOHN GOGARTY, *AS I WAS GOING
DOWN SACKVILLE STREET*

• • •

Delightful the path of sin/But a holy death's a habit.
Good man yourself there, Oscar/Every way you had it.
—BRENDAN BEHAN'S HOMAGE TO OSCAR WILDE

• • •

May you be in Heaven a full half hour before the
Devil knows you're dead.
—IRISH BLESSING

Last Words:

"¿Quién es? ¿Quién es?" ("Who is it? Who is it?")
—BILLY THE KID BEFORE BEING SHOT BY
SHERIFF PAT GARRETT

• • •

"That was a great game of golf, fellas."
—BING CROSBY BEFORE HE DROPPED DEAD ON THE 18TH HOLE

• • •

"Take a step forward lads—it'll be easier that way."
—ERSKINE CHILDERS IN FRONT OF A
FREE STATE FIRING SQUAD, 1922

• • •

"Shoot, coward. You are only going to kill a man."
—CHE GUEVARA

• • •

"Does nobody understand?"
—JAMES JOYCE

• • •

"Ah, well I suppose it has come to this… Such is life."
—NED KELLY, AUSTRALIAN OUTLAW

• • •

"It tastes bad."
—MARGARET MITCHELL

• • •

"Either that wallpaper goes or I do."
—OSCAR WILDE, DYING IN A PARIS BEDROOM

• • •

"I knew it. I knew it. Born in a hotel room—and
God damn it—died in a hotel room."
—EUGENE O'NEILL

• • •

Death

"Dying is easy; comedy is hard."
—GEORGE BERNARD SHAW

INDEX

Index